D1599719

Lichfield
CATHEDRAL
A Journey of Discovery

JONATHAN FOYLE

Size2
NA
5471
L5
F69
2016

I

CONTENTS

OPPOSITE
Lichfield's Lady
Chapel is remarkable
both for its intrinsic
beauty and for
its improbable
adoption of imported
sixteenth-century
glass during the
Georgian age.
Less obvious is
the political context
that informed its
distinctive Parisian
design.

PREVIOUS PAGE
The Hacket Window
in the south choir
aisle, by C.E. Kempe,
c.1901, detail showing
Bishop John Hacket
(1661–70) poring
over plans for the
rebuilding of his
cathedral, which had
been 'overthrown by
violent and wicked
hands' during the
Civil War.

OPPOSITE
The west front and
spires seen in late
afternoon sun from
the site where a
medieval gate once
stood, entry through
which made this view
yet more dramatic
for generations of
pilgrims.

BELOW RIGHT
A mural tomb
monument of an
unknown prelate,
given a prominent
position by the south
transept doors at the
end of the thirteenth
century.

PREVIOUS SPREAD
Lichfield Cathedral
once stood behind
a stone ring of
fortifications, built
during the twelfth
and thirteenth
centuries. After those
walls and gates were
levelled during the
Civil War, the north
bank of Minster Pool
gave rise to numerous
magnificent trees that
now frame views of
the cathedral.

Introduction

Why does Lichfield Cathedral stand here, its three sanguine stone spires reflected in Minster Pool? It is a familiar and picturesque view, one that has graced a million calendars. But it was not inevitably so, and for curious minds this fine urban panorama raises many questions.

As a visitor you will probably approach the cathedral from the south, by Dam Street and over its causeway, breaching a row of great trees. Why does the stump of a medieval turret stand to the right of this thoroughfare? As the unusually slender windows of the Lady Chapel rise ahead, you might ask why you have arrived in the close at the back of the great church, toward its east end, rather than at the main west doors. The cathedral is capped by crisp parapets: how much of the stonework is original, how much has been replaced, and what was changed in the process … isn't this the cathedral destroyed in the Civil War, then rebuilt?

Moving toward the west doors, you will encounter a weathered tomb monument in the south transept, and may notice that these walls show the scars and worn blocks of successive changes. Past the nave's unusual triangular windows comes the west front, a mighty cliff of fine Victorian statuary. Through its portals, a long vista opens up inside. And as your eyes adjust to the darkness you are left to inspect and interpret the cathedral's volumes and myriad details.

Many will appreciate the handsome proportions of the nave, much as they admired the spectacular effect of the west front. Few will be able to see the carefully sculpted details on the vault bosses. And no-one can behold the features that have long gone, whether bombarded, stripped out by reformers or scrubbed by over-zealous restorers. What were its generations

OPPOSITE
The west front,
rich with sculpture.
The main effect is
original to *c*.1300; the
details owe much to
Victorian restoration.

BELOW
The nave, which
greets visitors
with profound
atmosphere, superb
proportions and
refined details.

of creators trying to tell us through this great, multi-layered work of art? Lichfield Cathedral was bequeathed to us as the grand design of a committee that has long fallen silent, and we may not expect to distinguish the special reasons for their extraordinary efforts.

Lichfield seldom features in accounts of English cathedrals. This book attempts to redress this underestimation, through looking more closely than before at what the building tries to tell us when we set its visual language within a political and comparative context. Any attempt to reveal meaning demands an appreciation of the perceptions and values of the cathedral's makers, people whom we might instinctively think of as compatriots, but whose speech, ethics and beliefs we would today find quite alien. This commitment represents a journey through time, a process of discovery that challenges the familiar, asks us what we have inherited, and even what our own contemporary values represent by comparison.

That journey is well worth taking. Lichfield's specific role amongst English cathedrals may have been obscured for centuries, but this book argues that it is essentially recoverable. There are myriad ways of seeing this great church, and there is no substitute for experiencing the living history of Lichfield Cathedral for yourself.

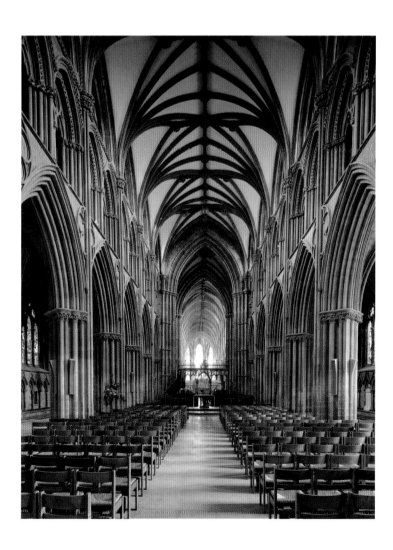

OPPOSITE
King Wulfhere, king
of Mercia 658–76,
shown on the west
front holding a model
of a church. St Chad
relocated the seat
of the Mercian
diocese from Repton,
Derbyshire, to
Lichfield before
St Peter's Church
was built *c.*700.
Wulfhere holds a
symbolic model of
the first church of
St Mary that Chad
had either inherited
or began to build.

BELOW RIGHT
West Stow Anglo-
Saxon village, Suffolk;
archaeological
reconstruction of a
typical settlement of
the early Anglo-Saxon
era, based on East
Anglian archaeology.

PREVIOUS SPREAD
The distant view
across Minster Pool,
with Lichfield's three
spires, the Ladies of
the Vale, dominating
the still-unspoilt
cathedral close.

I

Journey to the Heart of England

Lichfield Cathedral was founded around 670 CE – over 50 generations ago – when the kingdom of Mercia in which it emerged was a very different world to our own. The Roman empire had collapsed only two and a half centuries earlier, leaving Britannia to its fate, a northern outpost in a largely uncharted world. England was not yet a united country but a number of feuding kingdoms in fluid boundaries, with around two million people in all. Mercia lay in the middle of this island of settlers, bounded to the west and north by the native Cornish, Welsh and Scots, with separate languages and identities.[1] *None of these were urban societies. Tintagel in Cornwall was the principal trading post with the distant cities of the 'Middle Sea', beyond which was Jerusalem, then supposedly Eden, and the margins of the earth.*

In contrast to our own world of cheap saturated colour, the vivid hues were restricted to the rich embellishments of society's elite and to the natural jewellery of field flowers. Rural Mercia was built of timber and straw, its people dressed in linen beneath wool

or fur cloaks. They knew savage battles over territory, shared the relief of spring's warmth and early fruits and hoped that good harvests might save them from famine through the winter months. Theirs were hard, short lives, and many believed that a better future lay beyond.

St Augustine, the emissary of Pope Gregory the Great, had arrived in Kent to re-Christianize the Angles in 597, only 70 years before the foundation of Lichfield. Since then, the missionaries in his wake

had worked to persuade the English populace to accept their conviction that Christ's resurrection promised salvation, as a reward for prescribed moral conduct. In their huts, warmed and lit by flames, people told the tales of their ancestors, of the old gods, and some recalled biblical stories. Within their landscape rose monuments of timber or stone, resounding with theatre, voice and colourful imagery. These churches represented earth's portals to heaven, and their arts offered a glimpse to a life beyond – the eternal spring of Paradise or, indeed, the endless winter of Hell.

St Chad and his Times

A GILDED RELIQUARY IN ST CHAD'S CATHEDRAL, BIRMINGHAM, OSTENTATIOUSLY protects the remains of eight ancient bones. It was made in 1841 to the designs of the early Victorian architect A.W.N. Pugin and upholds the almost vanished tradition of English medieval great churches, whereby many thousands of pilgrims travelled

hundreds of miles to visit bejewelled containers of holy relics promising miraculous powers of salvation. These particular bones were not from Birmingham but from Lichfield. They are held to be those of St Chad, who died on 2 March 672 at Lichfield, where successive and multiple shrines for his limbs were venerated for almost nine hundred years.[2] Together, they are central to the story of a cathedral church that grew far beyond anything Chad could have conceived of in the late seventh century, and which continues to carry his name more than 1300 years beyond his lifetime.

Chad was born just after 630 CE in the kingdom of Northumbria, then comprising Deira from the Humber to the Tees, and Bernicia from the Tees to the Forth. The source for his life is the Venerable Bede who, in his *History of the Church in England*, described him with unusual respect, explaining that he was one of four brothers who were all clerics. Chad followed one of them, Cedd (who also became a saint), to study under the Irish St Aidan (*c*.590–651). Aidan had come from the important Celtic monastery of Iona to establish a monastic cathedral on the island of Lindisfarne, at the behest of King Oswald of Northumbria (r. 634–42). Oswald was the most powerful British ruler of his time and

OPPOSITE
The shrine to St
Chad in St Chad's,
Birmingham, both
shrine and cathedral
designed by A.W.N.
Pugin. Chad's bones
were installed on the
day of consecration,
21 June 1841. The
shrine was further
embellished by
Hardman & Co
in 1931.

RIGHT
Modern statue
of St Chad in his
eponymous parish
church in Lichfield,
holding aloft a model
of the fully developed
medieval cathedral
of which he was the
founder.

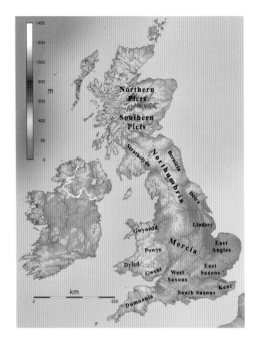

RIGHT
The Anglo-Saxon kingdoms in the seventh century.

BELOW LEFT
The seventh-century church of St John, Escomb, County Durham, typically northern in its tall proportions and simple, rectilinear form.

BELOW RIGHT
Ground plan of the important church at Reculver, Kent, founded in 669, the same year Chad moved his see to Lichfield. The central yellow plan represents the earliest building, its rounded apse, columnar screen and projecting cells all characteristic of the Roman manner imported in the wake of St Augustine, who arrived at Canterbury from Rome in 597.

was canonized after his death in battle against the pagan Penda of Mercia (d. 655).

During Chad's adolescence Mercia was beginning its 150 year-long expansion and was poised to adopt Christianity. In 653 the religion was accepted by Peada, king of Middle Anglia, the Fenland territory to the east of Mercia.[3] Following the example of Northumbrian (and Kentish) kings, Peada invested in new churches, notably Medes-hamsted (Peterborough) Abbey in 654. Its dedication to St Peter, the 'first pope' was specifically Roman, and of significance for Lichfield, as Peada became king of Mercia just two years later.

The adoption of Christianity as a state religion offered a clear political advantage for rulers, an internationally recognized legitimacy adhering to papal Rome and its imperial pedigree. Peada established his Mercian see at Repton in Derbyshire, where he was baptised. Yet there were two Christian cultures to reconcile. The Northumbrian Celtic church had evolved from an ascetic monasticism of contemplation and study in harsh natural environments, in contrast to the more cosmopolitan mysticism of Roman Catholicism, as established in England by Augustine in Canterbury from 597 and promoted by his missionaries. Northumbrian churches were plain, tall cells with a square chancel; broad Roman churches had columnar screens dividing public naves from rounded apses dressed with rich materials. Peada's contemporary, Oswiu of Northumbria, was sympathetic to the Roman cause. He founded Whitby Abbey in 657 and presided over the Synod of Whitby in 664, with the crucial involvement of Cedd, Chad's brother, as

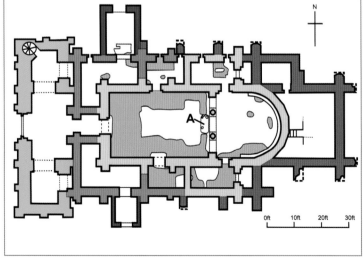

arbitrator. The result was the triumph of the Roman calendar and tonsure. Soon after, Chad was elevated to the bishopric of Northumbria, based at York, and then became the fifth bishop of Mercia.[4]

Herein lies a crucial question: why did Chad establish his seat in Lichfield in 669? There seem to be compounded reasons. In the mid-660s, plague was spreading; Chad's own brother Cedd fell victim to it.[5] When a populace is fearful, a leader's beliefs may be less persuasive and many Mercians may have feared that pestilence was a retribution for having abandoned their old gods. In dealing with this crisis in the few years before Chad's accession, King Wulfhere granted lands including Lichfield to St Wilfrid. In 709, Eddius Stephanus explained in his *Life of Wilfrid* that:

> Wilfrid knew of a place in the kingdom of Wulfhere, King of the Mercians, his faithful friend, which had been granted to him at Lichfield as it was suitable as an Episcopal see either for himself or any other to whom he might wish to give it. So a friendly arrangement was made with that true servant of God, Chad, who in all things obeyed the bishops. They thereupon consecrated him through all the ecclesiastical decrees. The King received him in an honourable manner and the bishops installed him in the said place.[6]

This 'suitability' must have been geographical. Lichfield was only 7.5 miles from Tamworth, the fortified administrative capital of Mercia, and was also near a Roman town, Letocetum. As a former Roman posting station, Letocetum lay closer to the intersection of Watling Street and Ryknield Street, with far better access to the road network than Repton had. Chad was a restless missionary on foot, but now his imperative was to minister to a turbulent populace from the heart of the kingdom. Hence the archbishop, Theodore of Tarsus, not only 'ordered him to ride whenever he was faced with too long a journey' but 'lifted him onto the horse'. Lichfield was a good strategic choice for an evangelist on horseback, especially as Chad's diocese included Lindsey (the area around Lincoln), reached via the Fosse Way. It is due to the combination of these political, social and practical reasons that Lichfield Cathedral came to be situated here.[7]

Chad did not settle at Letocetum, as Bede explains:

> Chad accepted the position as bishop of the Mercian race and of the people of Lindsey […] He had his Episcopal seat at a place called Lichfield […] (and) he built himself a more retired dwelling-place not far from the church, in which he could read and pray privately with a few of his brothers, that is to say seven or eight of them.

The term used for his dwelling was *mansio remotior*, which might be thought of as an oratory, harbouring the sort of isolated contemplation that Chad had learned from the ascetic St Aidan in Northumbria.[8] He very probably adopted an ancient British holy spring, like that which gave rise to Wells Cathedral.[9] In this case, it was situated by what is still called St Chad's Well.

Bede also explains that Chad's main public church was dedicated to St Mary, which was almost certainly on the site of the present cathedral. Though built of timber, it would be a mistake to assume it was insignificant. It was, after all, a *de facto* cathedral church with a bishop's throne, and it held important connotations. Mary's cult had been heralded by the Council of Ephesus in 431, and as the protectress of Constantinople she evolved into a militant figure, but as Christ's mother she was also the mediator of suffering between Christ and mankind. These Byzantine expressions were adopted in western thought and art during the Anglo-Saxon era.

We might wonder whether and how the earliest Lichfield Cathedral expressed such themes in art and furnishings. Comparison with an important seventh-century church built by Chad's contemporary and fellow Northumbrian, Benedict Biscop, may help. [10] Bede explains that Biscop returned from Rome in 674 laden with:

> Many holy pictures of the saints to adorn the church of St Peter he had built: a painting of the Mother of God, the blessed Mary ever-Virgin, and one each of the twelve apostles which he fixed round the central arch on a wooden entablature reaching from wall to wall; pictures of incidents in the gospels with which he decorated the south wall; and scenes from St John's vision of the apocalypse on the north wall. Thus all who entered the church, even those who could not read, were able, whichever way they looked, to contemplate the dear face of Christ and of his saints, even if only in a picture, to put themselves more firmly in mind of the Lord's incarnation and, as they saw the decisive moment of the Last Judgement before their very eyes be brought to examine their conscience with all severity.

The pestilence of the 660s took a number of Lichfield's earliest clergy, as Bede relates: 'A plague sent from heaven came upon them which, through the death of the body, translated the living stones of the church from their earthly sites to the heavenly building.' [11] This Petrine biblical phrase would resonate later in the Middle Ages. [12] But it is Bede's account of what happened to Chad in the last week of his life that would become central to Lichfield's mythology. He tells us that a brother called Owine approached Chad in his oratory on a winter's day, when he witnessed 'joyful song ascend from the roof of the oratory and return with unspeakable sweetness to the sky'. Chad explained to Owine that 'they were indeed angel spirits come to summon me to the heavenly joys which I have always loved and longed for'. Chad died after seven days, on 2 March 672. He was 'released from the prison-house of the body and in the company of angels, as one may rightly believe, sought the joys of heaven'.

A second church, dedicated to St Peter, was built by Bishop Hedda in December 700. Bede explains that Chad was 'first of all buried close to the church of St Mary; but when the church of St Peter [...] was later built, his bones were translated there [...] in each place frequent miracles of healing occur as a sign of his virtue'. Miracles could also be used to destroy the pagan idols 'or sometimes to confirm the faith of weak believers'. Chad's

THE STAFFORDSHIRE HOARD

ABOVE
Relics from seventh-century Mercia found in the Staffordshire hoard included a gold cross with pin holes and fastenings for gemstones typical of the dressings on Bible covers of this period.

RIGHT
The hoard also contained more martial equipment, notably this helmet cheek-piece, magnificently decorated with four bands of interlaced running animals.

On 5 July 2009, an astonishing discovery illuminated the turbulence of the era when Chad founded Lichfield Cathedral. In a field just off Watling Street three miles WSW of Lichfield, near the village of Hammerwich, an early Anglo-Saxon stash of 5 kg of gold was found.

The hoard comprised over 4,000 fragments of precious metals stripped from weapons, suggesting the removal of personal identity from the spoils of battle. They are dated to around 650 CE.[13] The metalcraft is of the highest quality, and its proximity to Tamworth and Lichfield, at the administrative heart of the Mercian kingdom, supports a royal provenance. Among the pieces were eight gold crosses, one folded, and a silver gilt strip inscribed with a Christian motto: 'Rise up, O Lord, and may thy enemies be scattered and those who hate thee be driven from thy face'.[14]

Several pieces from the hoard are displayed in the cathedral. The destruction of the crosses suggests the Mercian Church faced a struggle for ideology, but the circumstances of burial may never be known: the relics were hidden by those who would never return to collect them, whether by displacement, battle or illness.

bones were set in 'a wooden coffin in the shape of a little house, having an aperture in its side, through which those who visit it out of devotion can inset their hands and take out a little of the dust'.

A cathedral of two buildings may seem odd, but the dual dedication of separate churches of SS Mary and Peter was common in seventh-century England, at Exeter and Winchcombe for example. All such groups are gone, though St Augustine's Abbey in Canterbury, which was similar, still partly remains. The first churches at Lichfield were apparently aligned with the site of the oratory at what is still known as St Chad's church by Stowe Pool. Today, the closest comparator of the effect of multiple axially-aligned churches can be found 2,500 miles away, in the string of Romanesque monuments at Gelati in Georgia.

Bede's *History* remained a primary source of information on Lichfield. The dedications to St Mary and St Peter, the vision of angels through which Chad was heralded as a witness to heaven, his remains in a house-shaped shrine: through these, the seeds of the later medieval Lichfield Cathedral were sown. The remaining Anglo-Saxon story of Lichfield Cathedral is illuminated by the diversity and quality of surviving early arts that reveal its early cultural importance.

The Lichfield Gospels

THE ILLUMINATED CALLIGRAPHY OF GOSPEL MANUSCRIPTS REPRESENTS THE apogee of early British artistry, especially work from the fastidious Celtic traditions of Ireland and Lindisfarne. The Lichfield Gospels, also know as St Chad's Gospels, comprise the gospels of saints Matthew and Mark and the beginning of Luke. They have belonged to the cathedral since at least the tenth century, when an inscription in the margin records Wynsige as bishop of Lichfield, *c.*963–972/5. They were certainly unknown to St Chad, being written in around 730, over fifty years after his death.

The volume is illustrated with a rich carpet page, portraits of the evangelists Mark and Luke, decorated incipit pages (the beginning of the text), and a Chi-Rho monogram. It also has an inscription revealing that part of its early life was spent in Wales; this says that Gelhi bought it for the price of his best horse, to present it 'to God on the altar of St Teilo'. Teilo was a sixth-century Welsh saint, and further marginalia refer to parcels of land within 15 miles of the principal shrine church to St Teilo at Llandeilo Fawr in Carmarthenshire.

The book was made at some date between the Lindisfarne Gospels (*c.*700–15) and the Book of Kells (*c.*800), and the style of the illumination is so close to the Lindisfarne Gospels as to show that the scribe must have studied them. Celtic culture is as strange to Welsh traditions as it is to the typically Anglo-Saxon runic script.

OVERLEAF
Lichfield Cathedral viewed from St Chad's church, the probable site of St Chad's oratory. The near-alignment of the two buildings betrays an axial relationship typical of Anglo-Saxon churches.

On balance, it seems that a Celtic scribe made the book for Lichfield and that it was plundered from there during the eighth century. If that is correct, the volume was returned to Lichfield after Llandeilo waned as a spiritual centre, by the end of the ninth century. But who then could have known its origins were at Lichfield? Presumably, it was labelled in some way.

In 2014 specialist imaging revealed three female names added to the margins, showing that Lichfield's late Saxon scriptorium was at least partly populated by women. We can be sure that the Gospels have been at Lichfield for over a thousand years, and it is the book upon which Lichfield's bishops swear allegiance to the Crown. But they are only a part-survival; for most of their existence, they were accompanied by a second volume, which was apparently lost during the chaos of the Civil War. Early notes at the foot of the existing volume suggest its division happened in Wales.

ABOVE
The Lindisfarne Gospels clearly influenced the Lichfield Gospels, which were made not much more than a generation later.

OPPOSITE
The Lichfield Gospels on display in the cathedral.

Lichfield Cathedral

THE ST. CHAD GOSPELS

dating from c730AD

IN LOVING MEMORY OF
ARTHUR STRETTON REEVE
BISHOP OF LICHFIELD
1953-1974

The Lichfield Angel

KING OFFA OF MERCIA (757–96) IS FAMOUS FOR THE EPONYMOUS DITCH spanning the Welsh borders from the Severn to the Irish Sea, by which he defended his kingdom from Wales.[15] A further testament to his ambition is his decree of around 787, when Mercia was at its greatest extent, having conquered East Anglia, Kent, and Wessex, that Lichfield should be an archiepiscopal see, freed of the jurisdiction of the archbishop of Canterbury.[16]

These years before 800 CE coincided with a revival of classical arts in the service of the Church across northern Europe. This 'Carolingian Renaissance' was named after Charles the Great ('Charlemagne'), who was crowned the first Holy Roman Emperor at Christmas 800 CE, and who fostered a self-consciously imperial court in Aachen, Germany.[17] In Mercia, numerous ecclesiastical sculptures testify to the high artistic quality of central England.

A spectacular discovery in 2003 revealed Lichfield Cathedral's distinctive contribution to the Carolingian Renaissance. An excavation beneath the nave floor found Anglo-Saxon foundations, perhaps those of the Archbishop Hygeberht's cathedral. These in turn probably also marked the site of the first church of St Peter around the shrine of St Chad, which remained the focus of successive rebuildings. Face-down on rubble over a dry void lay an extremely fine, broken bas-relief sculpture of an angel, dating from the turn of the ninth century; beneath it was a coin of King Edgar (957–75). These foundations, the crypt-like void and smashed sculpture together cast some light on Dark Age Lichfield.

The three surviving fragments of the 'Lichfield Angel' are made from Ancaster limestone, quarried near Grantham in the Roman era, which points to salvage via the River Trent or from Letocetum. Together the fragments constitute half of a monumental coffin-cover, or the facing slab of a gable-fronted shrine casket: Bede's description of the first shrine as

LEFT
The Lichfield Angel is an exceptional work of art, rediscovered beneath the nave in 2003, over a millennium after its burial. This depiction of Gabriel's annunciation to Mary of the birth of Christ includes a plant tendril, a shoot of new life symbolizing the redemptive promise of the story of Christ.

'house-shaped' recalls the origins of the gable, as shrines and many tombs represented heavenly mansions with roofs. The figure is the archangel Gabriel, who appeared to Mary, as described in St Luke's gospel.[18] His annunciation of her virgin conception was the start of the redemption story, leading through Christ's birth, death and resurrection to the triumph over death and the recovery of paradise.

The angel was painted with colours, some of which remarkably survive: purple, red, black and white, the wing feathers shaded with sophisticated graduation. Mary is missing from the scene, but she was undoubtedly on the lost right-hand side of the panel. This choice of imagery says much about the strength of Mary's identity at Lichfield; as co-dedicatee, her representation flourishes in the arts throughout the Middle Ages.

Hygeberht's career as archbishop lasted only a decade, but Lichfield's metropolitan status is unlikely to have been forgotten quickly, although its history becomes obscure to us.[19] A century on, in 873–74, the town was struck by a Viking raid that swept across north-west Mercia. We can only imagine what was destroyed in the cathedral. This might seem the likeliest occasion for a sacking to wreck the shrine and smash the figure of Gabriel, yet the angel's interment came a hundred years later, in the late tenth century. So it may be that it survived the Vikings because, whether part of a shrine or a tomb, carved stone had no material value. The Gabriel figure was carefully – apparently reverently – laid face down in the aftermath of its destruction to make way for its replacement.

The revival of Lichfield Cathedral with a new shrine was a likely response to St Dunstan's monastic reforms, which revived English great churches in the period before the Norman Conquest. Dunstan was archbishop of Canterbury from 960, and was renowned for his skill in scribing, painting and metalwork as much as for the management by which he brought monks into many cathedrals and asserted rules for canons. The recovery of Lichfield and the celebration of its artistic glories under Dunstan as its primate – Lichfield falling under Canterbury rather than York – could account for a finer shrine and also explain the arrival, or perhaps return, of the Lichfield Gospels coincident with the earliest Lichfield name

BELOW
All Saints' Church, Brixworth, Northamptonshire. The arcades now visible led into side-chapels called 'porticus', now removed. With them in place, and minus its spire, this basilica-style building, a large Mercian church of the ninth and tenth centuries, represents a comparator for Lichfield Cathedral, though the cathedral probably had a central tower and transepts.

in its margins, Bishop Wynsige, who ruled in the years before 975. The nearby abbey of Breedon-on-the-Hill was rebuilt at this time. If Lichfield Cathedral were indeed remodelled, we might look to Brixworth in Northamptonshire, and the crypt at Repton, for comparators.

Untold thousands of pilgrims came to this treasure house to see Chad's shrine, served by generations of its customary five priests, who under successive bishops rebuilt, refurbished and embellished the churches that Chad himself had founded.

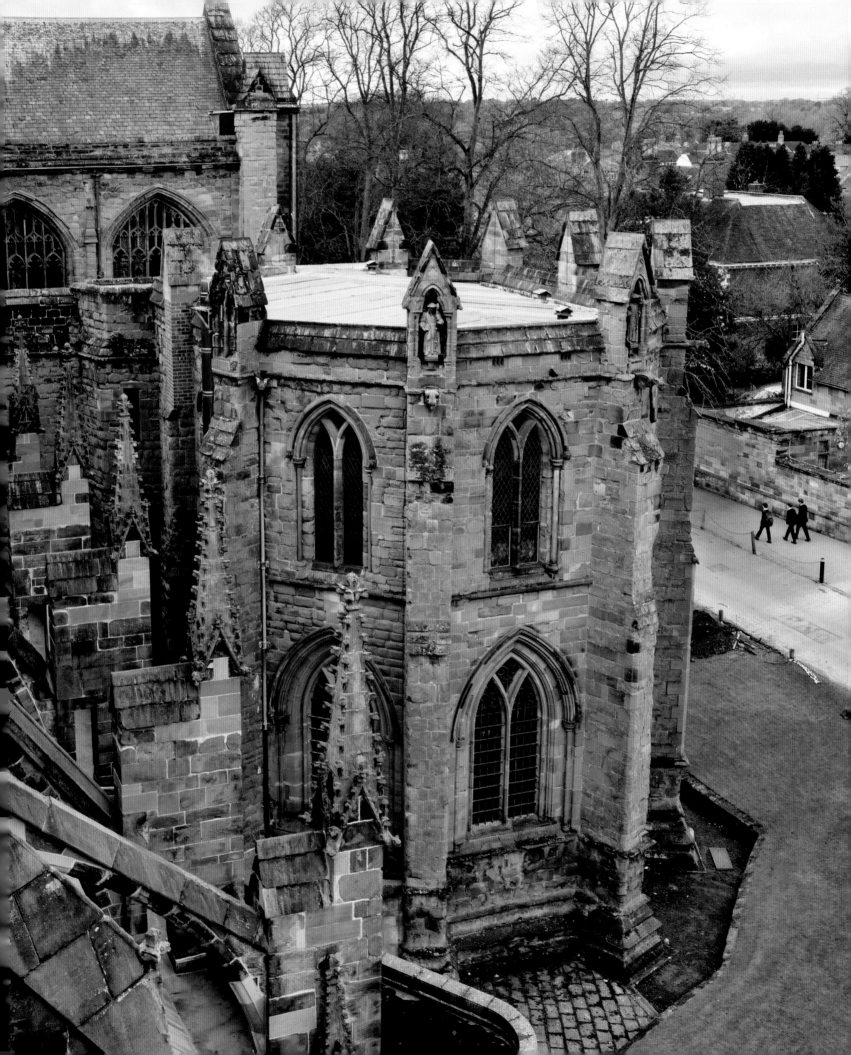

OPPOSITE

The distinctive two-storey chapter house and muniment room viewed from the east. It was completed by around 1250.

RIGHT

St Peter's Basilica, Rome; the fourth-century layout shows the apse, bema (transept) and five-aisled nave. Over the following seven centuries, northern European builders transformed this essential model into a typically three-aisled nave, a crossing tower over the transept, which was separated from the apse by a choir, and a western block and/or towers.

PREVIOUS SPREAD

The concept and details of the mid-thirteenth-century nave of Lichfield Cathedral were based on exemplars: Sainte-Chapelle in Paris, Westminster Abbey and Lincoln Cathedral. The majority of the original vaults were replaced by remarkably convincing late-eighteenth-century replicas.

2

The Arrival of the Kings' Bishops

William of Normandy's short voyage across the English Channel in 1066 led to a lasting change in the way English cathedrals were designed. In contrast to what were often several small churches with compartmented volumes strung along an east-west axis, the religious power-houses of the Norman overlords were monumental, evoking the imperial grandeur of ancient Rome. The firm basis of Norman cathedral design was the 'basilica', the ancient Roman hall with arcades forming aisles, which had offered a prototype for the naves of larger churches during the early Christian centuries, and rounded 'apses' to house altars. This influential shape spread far beyond the fourth-century Christian Emperor Constantine's archetypal St Peter's basilica, which also included a transept

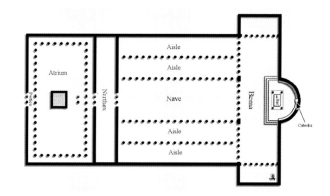

known as a 'bema'. Some of the greater Anglo-Saxon churches sympathetic to Rome had already joined this tradition of basilican design with transepts – England saw the first Norman-styled great church in Edward the Confessor's Westminster Abbey even before the Conquest – but the regime of William I developed the tradition on a hitherto unknown scale. It could only be achieved by sweeping away the existing cathedrals.

Bishop Leofwin, the last Anglo-Saxon bishop of Lichfield, was installed in Lichfield in 1053. He submitted to the Norman Conquest and to the new king from 1066, but his days were numbered. If being a nephew of the Saxon Earl Leofric and Countess Godgifu (Godiva) was not cause enough to question his loyalties, he was also married, which met with the

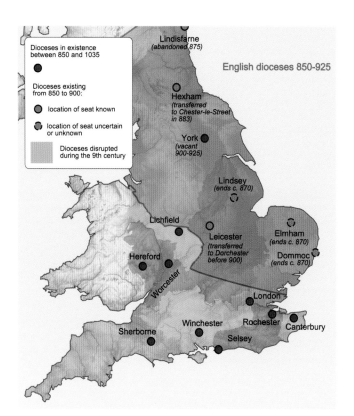

FAR LEFT
Map showing
the locations of
later Anglo-Saxon
cathedrals and their
dioceses.

LEFT
William the
Conqueror (1066–87)
as envisaged on the
west front of Lichfield
Cathedral.

reproof of the new Norman primate of England, Lanfranc of Canterbury. Leofwin retired to Coventry, where he died in around 1070. This made way for Bishop Peter, possibly a royal chaplain, to accede to Lichfield in 1072, just in time for his attendance at the Council of London around Easter 1075.[20] The council's decree that bishoprics were no longer to be situated in petty towns like Dorchester-on-Thames, Thetford or Selsey, was the making of cities such as Lincoln, Norwich and Chichester. Lichfield, however, then centered on the Cross Keys and Lombard Street area, was judged an insignificant settlement.[21]

> By the decrees of Popes Damasus and Leo, and by the Councils of Sardica and Laodicea, bishops' sees should not be in vills, they should be in cities so the Council agreed that three bishops should migrate from vills to cities – those moved were Herman from Sherborne to Salisbury, Peter from Lichfield to Chester and Stigand from Selsey to Chichester.

So Peter of Lichfield became bishop of Chester.[22] Though he was not of the political first division, he would do the king's bidding and Chester was strategically powerful, situated by the Welsh border and with access to the Irish Sea. It also had a reputation of being 'anciently known as the City of Legions' (according to William of Malmesbury), and it could therefore combine church and castle against potential rebellion, like Durham or Lincoln. But what did this manoeuvring mean for Lichfield Cathedral? Was it now no longer a cathedral, but simply a church of priests, with an illustrious mythology and the dim memory of an early monastery?

The new episcopal title for the diocese seems uncertain; a Canterbury memorandum of c.1073–75 refers to 'the Bishop of Lichfield who is now Chester' rather than 'the Bishop of Chester who was Lichfield', a slight but significant difference that upholds Lichfield's identity.[23] To add to the confusion, another church had to be factored in – St Mary's Coventry, a monastery in a new town, recently endowed by Leofric and Godgifu/Godiva. This tripartite arrangement remained in some flux, as between 1089 and 1102 the bishop's seat at Chester moved again, not back to Lichfield but on to Coventry, which was re-consecrated as a cathedral priory in 1102. One might assume that, as the bishop was now simply 'bishop of Coventry', Lichfield had been relegated.

Surprisingly, however, it seems to have remained business as usual at Lichfield throughout the total replacement of its architecture. Domesday Book tells us that its five canons upheld their five prebends, in an apparently long tradition, and ploughed on (literally, with three ploughs between them). It was they who still held services at the high altar.[24] The absence of a bishop may not have been much of an issue. At Coventry the presence of a bishop was resisted by the monks in the twelfth century, while the building of episcopal inns in London ensured that more of the bishops' time was spent in the capital, to serve the affairs of the royal court.

Perhaps the best way to account for Lichfield's apparent lack of demotion is to correlate Chester, Coventry and Lichfield as serving specific functions within the diocese. The historian Chris Lewis suggests that this unique tripartite arrangement upheld the original roles of Chad's three early churches, even respecting their original dedications, with Chester as cathedral (St Peter), Coventry as monastery (St Mary) and Lichfield as oratory (Holy well/St Chad's chapel-of-ease and shrine church). This would reflect an exceptional respect for ancient customs in an age of royal Norman prerogative over church affairs. What is certain is that none of these foundations was abandoned; to the contrary, each was invested with rebuilding.

Building Work, 1066–1200

THE GREATEST CHANGE TO LICHFIELD WAS THAT ITS STRING OF ANGLO-SAXON churches went the way of all others, to be utterly replaced. A Norman basilican church was begun sometime between 1085 and 1100, under Bishop Robert de Limesey (1085–1117), another possible royal chaplain. His builders found bedrock 2 m (7 ft) down, and used sandstone quarries to the south of the city for their building supplies.

Nothing obvious of this first Norman church remains above ground. The documentary history is absent and physical evidence is scant for the entire building before the thirteenth century. What we know relies on footings that came to light in two excavations: fragments of the east end found in 1856–60, during the restorations of George Gilbert Scott, which were observed but not completely understood by the great cathedral historian Robert

Willis; the footings of a wall associated with the Norman west front between the present towers; and further traces beneath the nave found in 2003, during excavations directed by the former cathedral archaeologist, Warwick Rodwell. In 1986–89 Rodwell suggested a revised evolution of the east end, from a rounded shape, perhaps with bubble-shaped chapels like Norwich, through several stages, into a square termination.

The simplicity of this building was not a reflection of Lichfield's only quasi-cathedral status; some major Benedictine abbey churches like Peterborough, Glastonbury and Bury St Edmunds were as grand and finely detailed as any cathedral. The local economy is the likely culprit for Lichfield was not affluent, being situated in a relatively poor diocese. As the centuries passed the city's trade grew, yet it remained overshadowed by Coventry and Chester's mercantile riches. They, however, could not touch Lichfield for its air of sanctity, nor match its prestigious situation in a royal forest.

In the turbulent years toward the middle of the twelfth century, Roger de Clinton built on Lichfield's reputation. In 1129 he became not only 'Bishop of Coventry' but 'Bishop of Lichfield and Coventry' and sometimes 'Bishop of Lichfield'. He was the nephew of Geoffrey de Clinton, a courtier of Henry I, who received estates to the south of

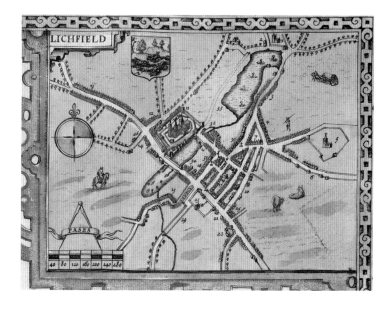

Lichfield forfeited by the earl of Warwick. Roger's nepotistic advancement brought a reforming character and keen builder to Lichfield; he set out the surviving ladder plan of Lichfield's streets, replacing the focus of the Anglo-Saxon settlement around Stowe Street. The close and the city were united by this plan, with the streets framing the sides of the ladder – Bird Street to the west and Dam Street to the east, which visitors still follow today – serving as Roger's access roads to his cathedral, while the roads linking them run more or less parallel with the cathedral.

OPPOSITE

The cathedral from the south-east; Lichfield never grew in size to rival Chester or Coventry.

RIGHT

John Speed's map of Lichfield, made in c.1610, showing the ladder of streets set out by Bishop Roger Clinton in the early twelfth century, which still remains the basis of the city centre today.

Lichfield proved a suitable town for a Sunday market, and as a third of the properties were owned by the cathedral, commerce directly benefited its coffers.[25] Roger de Clinton also reformed the cathedral chapter of canons, following Lincoln, York and Salisbury, perhaps to bolster Lichfield's standing against that of the monastic cathedral of Coventry. But Lichfield was distinctive, for it was modelled on the Institutions of Rouen.[26]

Bishop Roger's personal devotions are revealed through his patronage of two buildings dedicated to the Virgin Mary, whose cult was at the height of fashion in the middle of the twelfth century. Roger lived in an era when architecture still evoked Mary's persona as a protectress, the maternal figure with an impenetrable womb who was shown as the *hortus conclusus*, or defended garden.[27] Beyond Marian castle chapels, this was expressed in the

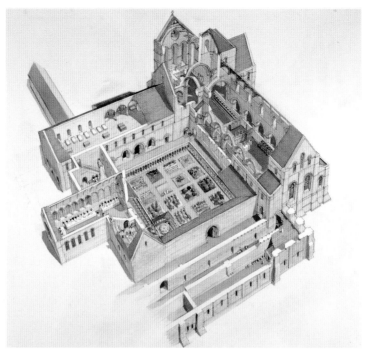

FAR LEFT
The Virgin, seen here in a fifteenth-century Paduan triptych, in her role as maternal protectress and intercessor between the realms of earth and paradise.

LEFT
Reconstruction of Buildwas Abbey, Shropshire, founded by Bishop Roger de Clinton. Cistercian churches had their own characteristic arrangement of short, squared chancel and monastic building, but Bishop Roger's foundation gives us an idea of scale of Lichfield Cathedral by the twelfth century, before the choir was lengthened and the spires added. Lichfield was unimpeded by monastic buildings.

fortified cathedral of St Mary's Lincoln (its castellar west front of c.1080) and possibly in Lichfield's partner cathedral, St Mary's Coventry, which was defended by a ditch in preparation for a siege in 1143. In an extension of this idea of a Marian paradise, the Virgin was popularly cast as the Queen of Heaven and both mother and bride of Christ ('*Ecclesia*'), the Lady of Sorrows, who suffered on behalf of mankind as her son was crucified.

New strands of Marian culture had recently been developed by several leading theologians. Anselm of Canterbury (1033–1109) upheld her as the paragon of sainthood (although he was never formally canonized, a relic of 'Saint' Anselm was recorded in Lichfield's sacristy in 1345). Later, St Bernard of Clairvaux (1090–1153), the founder in 1115 of the ascetic Cistercian rule, identified the Virgin as the subject of the biblical 'Song of Songs', and all Cistercian abbeys were dedicated to Mary. Bishop Roger founded a Cistercian house at Buildwas in Shropshire in 1135, and sometime after this, he may again have built in honour of the Virgin at Lichfield Cathedral, through the redevelopment of the original small, rounded east end.

Bishop Roger founded Lichfield's Lady Chapel in the years approaching his death (he died on 16 April 1148 at Antioch, during an arduous pilgrimage to Jerusalem). An axial chapel with an altar to the Virgin had been customary in the eastern ends of many cathedrals, but this concept was now being expanded into entire, often square-ended, buildings. And so it was at Lichfield, as trenches were dug for a three-bay Lady Chapel to replace the eastern apse, creating a block of around 40 ft (12 m) length, which curiously veered to the south. Humble origins, indeed, but this would evolve into one of the very finest Lady Chapels in the country.

The change came fast. Within a couple of decades – around 1170 – a whole new

rectangular choir with four eastern altars was built in its place. The scant remains of the new work can be seen in some of the typical 'waterleaf' capitals found toward the west end of the south choir aisle. Other traces of it – two blocked arches and a window embrasure above – are still visible within the choir's south wall, being trapped by the tower against them. After the 1170s choir arose, building work was constant, to the extent that the cathedral as we know it is essentially a thirteenth- and fourteenth-century creation (with additions and restorations, as we will see). The 1170s choir was probably not finished above 20 years when it was remodelled in turn. By now, Wells and Canterbury were England's major experiments in cathedral building, developing the early 'Gothic' style we associate with pointed arches, multiplied mouldings, and thin, applied shafts. But they offered distinctive approaches, and Lichfield fell under the spell of Wells, to judge from the three western bays of the rebuilt choir arcades, all that is left.[28] The timing of the rebuild may relate to 6 April 1192, when this church was chosen by John, count of Mortain, as a chantry to support prayers for his soul.[29] Seven years later, he became the notorious King John.

ABOVE
The two westernmost bays of the choir arcades from c.1190 follow the model of Wells Cathedral. The addition of the internal parapet and (restored) figures in niches belongs to the 1330s remodelling.

Thirteenth Century

THE YEARS AFTER 1200 SAW THE TYRANNICAL RULE OF KING JOHN (1199–1216) lead to the barons' wars, even as reforming thinkers such as Archbishop Stephen Langton of Canterbury and builders such as Bishop Richard Poore, the founder of Salisbury Cathedral, strengthened the independence of the Church from royal interference. Purgatory became an accepted idea, changing popular belief regarding the hope of salvation through intercessory prayers. Many of the oak and daub houses in Lichfield's new streets looked across Minster Pool to the unfinished cathedral, clad in timber scaffolding. Freshly quarried sandstone arrived for cutting, the masons' signed blocks hauled up by pulleys to be laid onto wet mortar. It would take over a century yet – many generations in Lichfield – for the cathedral to reach its essential form. And during that time, Lichfield Cathedral developed a story about its ancient origins that found expression in its architecture, and drew royal favour.

Now began 'the most rapid advance in the cathedral's history' when 'the chapter grew in wealth, independence and influence.'[30] Progress had already been made in 1166 with a lead-piped water supply from the eponymous Pipe, which once gushed at a rate of 128 gallons per hour from 2.3 km eastward to a reservoir in the north-west corner of the cathedral close. A medieval conduit head at Pipe Park (Maple Hays) survives, though the reservoir was abandoned after 800 years of use, in January 1969.[31]

In 1191 Bishop Hugh Nonant made Lichfield the first cathedral to be governed by fixed statutes, rather than ordinances and customs. Nonant may or may not have said 'I call my clerks gods and the monks demons' in his attempt to remove the monastery from Coventry Cathedral.[32] But the idea that Coventry might follow the model of Lichfield as a well-governed secular cathedral was a likely influence on the creation of a joint diocese in 1224. Physically, the church was growing to fulfil that role.

Lichfield's new crossing (with a tower or steeple) was an intrinsic part of the choir rebuilding. The crossing and transepts played an important role as a fitting threshold to the east end, which included the feretory containing Chad's main shrine. Transepts hosted altars, and now both the transept chapels gave way to a subdivided aisle providing a larger area. Structurally, it would be difficult to rebuild any limb of a great church adjacent to an existing crossing tower while maintaining the tower's stability. The massiveness of these great crossing piers implies the intention for a tower, even a spire. The piers' shafts, with regularly set rings, are typical of the turn of the thirteenth century.

Internally, the transepts have since been heavily remodelled; the best-surviving bays flank the eastern crossing piers, allowing us to attempt a reconstruction. They were of two storeys, so similar to the chapter house at Chester as to suggest the same designer. There is also a striking similarity between Chester and the five-light window in the

OPPOSITE
The north transept features restored five-light windows which complement the verticality of the applied shafts on the crossing tower piers. The two-storey arrangement, without the typically unlit central 'triforium' storey, created an unusually light interior.

The chapter house of Chester Cathedral was probably built by the team who worked on Lichfield's transepts, as much of the arrangement and details are directly comparable.

northern transept, as correctly restored. A similar arrangement was probably once also found beneath the rose window of the south transept.

The north and south doors of the transepts are exceptionally rich, with a trumeau (central column), more typical of France than England. The north door survives better than the south; even so, it has long been too worn to decipher, though Thomas Pennant, whom Samuel Johnson admired for his keen eye, valiantly attempted it two centuries ago:

> The northern door is extremely rich in sculptured moldings; three of foliage, and three of small figures in ovals. In one of the lowest is represented a monk baptizing a person kneeling before him. Probably the former is intended for *St. Chad*; the latter for *Wulferus*.[33]

The completion of the transepts proceeded through an age of turbulence. The Magna Carta years led to the reforming of the Church so that there could be no misunderstanding about the extent of royal jurisdiction – as in 1214, when King John had imposed his own choice of dean, Ralph Nevill, here. Some churches of this era became highly theatrical, to win hearts and minds; the grand screen façade of Wells was dense with painted biblical statuary. Others, like the interior of Salisbury, adopted the soberly authoritative aesthetic

The wheel window
in the south transept;
the arch mouldings
in front of the window
seem so low here as to
obscure the window,
but the ensemble was
intended to be seen
from the ground,
before the stone
vaults were inserted
in the middle of the
fourteenth century.
The window itself is
a seventeenth-century
replacement.

FAR RIGHT
The door of the
north transept, its
original, richly-carved
masonry surviving
comparatively well in
a sheltered position.

OVERLEAF
The view into the
much-rebuilt Head
Chapel from the
choir. Here, Chad's
skull was kept in
a portable shrine.
The fourteenth-
century gallery
that accompanied
the rebuilding
of the choir after
c.1337 has tracery
to complement
the eastern Lady
Chapel windows
that probably held
a crucifixion scene.
The gallery allowed
the relic to be
publicly displayed on
principal feast days,
in a broad cult of
martyrdom developed
at Lichfield.

of the Cistercian monasteries. Lichfield had been caught up in the building boom when, in 1221, the pope agreed it could elect its own dean. Substantial progress by that year is suggested by royal support; Henry III made a gift to Lichfield Cathedral of 20 oaks from Cannock Forest for rafters and timber. It is likely that these were sawn into beams and boards for roofing the choir, and the completion of the transepts followed when, in 1231, the king provided timber from Ogley Hay.

Henry III's contribution of building materials was reflected in his desire to emulate the 'new work at Lichfield' at St George's Chapel, Windsor, in 1242, with timber vaults painted in imitation of stonework. It is clear that Lichfield's transepts were indeed originally vaulted in timber, arching right up to the rafters to clear the wheel window in the south transept gable, now pointlessly adorning the roofspace. Its tracery was replaced in the seventeenth century, but the perimeter mouldings remain. These, and the inner round framing arch with pointed side arches, were designed as an ensemble, to be appreciated from within the building at floor level. This abnormally elevated wheel window, and five northern lancets opposite, once resembled the arrangement of the much bigger timber-vaulted transepts of York Minster, but remarkably Lichfield came first, which suggests the influential power of royal patronage.

In April 1224 Lichfield's status changed; it became a joint diocese, its title formally shared with Coventry, which led to their shared voting on bishops from 1228. The Head Chapel Tower to the south of the choir was rebuilt at this time, with a vaulted treasury below. The duties of the treasurer included not only the custody of precious objects but also responsibility for the candle lighting of the cathedral and, with the sacrist, the provision of bread, wine, incense, water, coals and rushes. The prominence of this store of riches on the south side of the choir may be partly explained by Lichfield's use of the Institutions of Rouen, which prioritized the treasurer above the precentor. Above the treasury store stood St Peter's Chapel at ground level; above this, was St Chad's Head Chapel. This arrangement upheld the Anglo-Saxon dedications, and while the east end was redeveloped in honour of Mary, the main shrine to Chad remained focal behind the high altar.

This rebuilt Head Chapel Tower may have been conceived by Dean William Mancetter, who had arrived in 1222. Now that Lichfield could elect its own deans, a chapter house of sorts must have been provided for them. By 1224, Mancetter was joined by the new bishop of Coventry and Lichfield, Alexander de Stavensby, his name (from 'Stainsby')

betraying a Lincolnshire man, who likely witnessed the rebuilding of Lincoln Cathedral after 1192 as a shrine church.[34] Stavensby, a well-travelled theologian and diplomat for Henry III, was in the circle of another Lincolnshire native, Stephen Langton, cardinal archbishop of Canterbury 1207–28.[35] Langton was the foremost English cleric of his time, credited with organizing the Latin Vulgate Bible into its current arrangement of chapters, and with steering Magna Carta. Since 1170 Canterbury had presided over the remains of Thomas Becket; it now had four shrines, but only in 1220 was Becket's principal shrine installed, with the separate expression of head and body. Canterbury's monks had also quite recently begun to trade on its early Saxon origins, with special interest in the graves and shrines of its founders, which lent a venerable antiquity that appealed to a papacy endeavouring to maintain the status quo in the face of episcopal reforms.[36] Both the culture of dividing the remains of a saint into separate shrines, and the study and uses of native history, would be freshly asserted at Lichfield. Here, the major historical source was Bede, and his authority was taken literally.

This tower structure presents an enigma. In 1981 a skeleton was discovered in an unmarked tomb set within the tower's south wall, at about head height. It proved to be William Mancetter, who must have made special provision for being walled up at his death in 1254. His example is not unique, however, for unusual elevated wall monuments of recumbent figures are found elsewhere at a similar height.[37]

There is one more tantalizing glimpse of Lichfield's embellishment in around 1240. A fragment of arcaded sculpture 1 m wide x 56 cm tall was recorded 'in [the Lady] chapel behind the choir' in 1702, and shown in a drawing made by the clergyman and antiquarian

OPPOSITE & LEFT The thirteenth-century Head Chapel was crushed by the falling masonry of the spire during the Civil War siege. Its rebuilding did not disturb the inter-mural burial of a skeleton identified as Dean William Mancetter.

WILLIAM de MANECESTRA

DEAN 1222-1254

William Stukeley.[38] It can only be a fragment of the base of St Chad's shrine, and shows two kings beneath trefoils: one sits cross-legged; the other is God crowning Mary.[39] Angels occupy the spandrels and the capitals are formed of concentric rings, much like those in the vestibule of the chapter house. This tells us that the identity of Chad's cathedral continued to be associated with Mary, and this earliest scene of her coronation becomes a prevalent theme in the cathedral's later sculpture.

The Chapter House

WHATEVER SUFFICED FOR A CHAPTER HOUSE UP TO THE MIDDLE OF THE thirteenth century was completely replaced by a two-storey building, which was in progress by 1249. Its shape, an octagon stretched on its west-east axis, is one of two unique features, the other its upper muniment room, with a secondary tiled floor, one of the finest in England, dating from c.1400.[40]

Lichfield's palm-vaulted polygon had been begun by the mid-1240s, when the major exemplar was Lincoln Cathedral's decagonal chapter house, dating from 1192 but still incomplete at 1220.[41] Several years prior to Stavensby's 1224 election to Lichfield, an exceptional text was written that described the architecture of Lincoln Cathedral. *The Metrical Life of St Hugh* tells how the chapter house presents a character that 'never Roman roof possessed' and has a kind of portico.[42] This is a clear reference to the greatest Roman vaulted roof, that of the Pantheon, essentially a spherical volume, its inner circumference punctuated by eight niches.[43] Lincoln's solid central vaulting, like Lichfield's, is the structural opposite of the Pantheon's open oculus. Importantly, the Pantheon's Christian rededication was to the Virgin Mary, an identity shared by Lincoln and Lichfield. So perhaps Lichfield followed the example of Lincoln's one-upmanship over Rome's ancient, subsequently Marian, monument.

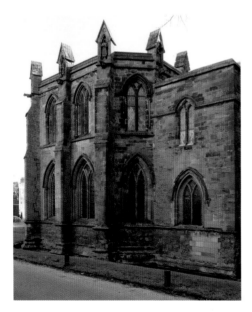

Lichfield's chapter house is approached by a rib-vaulted vestibule that reveals a degree of incoherence in its two side walls. The north exterior wall shows the octangular and rectangular buildings united by only a single moulding beneath the lower windows, while the window jambs are not uniform, suggesting revised intentions under new direction. The vestibule seems to be built up to a pre-existing buttress on the west face of the chapter house. Inside the vestibule, the east wall shows an external type of sloping plinth moulding beneath its arcade, the latter in turn carries a chunky sill, and above this springs a stone vault that has had to navigate abandoned wall openings relating to the intramural staircase. On the west side, however, there is no external plinth moulding, the taller arcade incorporates 13 stone

TOP

The 13-bay
pedilavium, raised
seating in the chapter
house vestibule,
dating from the
early 1240s.

ABOVE

The muniment room
with tiled floor.

seats within its arches, and here the vault has no pre-existing features to avoid. All this shows that the west side and the vault were an addition to the slightly earlier east wall, the original intention being to build a timber pentice, its roof beams lying on the east wall's sill.

Why the change of mind to incorporate raised seating? Evidence suggests the expectation of a royal visit at Easter. The earliest record of the Maundy Thursday ceremony of royal foot-washing in imitation of Christ was that by King John on 15 April 1210, not at Westminster but at Knaresborough, within another strategically important royal forest, where John washed 13 poor men's feet; and we have seen that John established a personal interest in Lichfield through his chantry.[44] John's son, Henry III, not only made a gift of timber to Lichfield Cathedral, he also visited this church within its royal forest three times, in 1235, 1237 and 1241. So in the early 1240s, a change of plan to incorporate a pedilavium with 13 seats would have constituted a wise precaution should a further royal visit to Lichfield happen at Easter.

ABOVE

The revised inclusion
of the pedilavium
inspired the vaulted
enclosure of the
vestibule space,
thwarting prepared
openings in the east
wall.

OPPOSITE TOP LEFT
The ornately decorated portal to the chapter house.

OPPOSITE TOP RIGHT
The central figure of Christ the judge in the trumeau above the chapter house portal.

OPPOSITE BELOW
The vaulted octagonal space of the chapter house contains rich, though much-restored, arcading, yet still retaining many traces of medieval painted decoration.

The vestibule's sculpture has suffered – how extraordinary, then, is the survival of the seated figure of Christ in Majesty in the tympanum of the vastly complex arch into the chapter house. As we enter its space, the octagonal form is clear, a central pier with rings of abundant stiff-leaf carving supporting fountain-like vault ribs. The room's perimeter arcade, once framing the canons' seats, features sculpted capitals with a variety of themes, almost all of which have been restored or replaced. The richest and most intact capitals frame the dean's seat. One shows a cat which has caught a mouse; hell was often shown as a cat's mouth, and in manuscripts cats were frequently coupled with owls, light-hating night hunters then also associated with Jews. A squirrel also features, to convey pregnancy, as it is the creature that ingests acorns (also shown), a symbol of male fertility. A bird may be the eagle of St John, whose attributed gospel of Revelation portrays the Last Judgment, promising paradise for the faithful. The scene is set amid fertile stiff-leaf foliage and single- and double-petalled roses, the earliest example of a Marian rose at Lichfield, an exceptionally important, and usually overlooked, motif. The combination of symbols suggests that the devilish cat is answered by Mary's pregnancy and, thereby, the advent of Christ – grapes representing his blood – and the return to the heavenly garden. Above the capitals are two busts, one female and one male, possibly Mary and Christ, and perhaps a God the Father to the right (south). They, in turn, would explain Christ's presence as judge over the doorway. In chapter meetings, the dean sat beneath the canopy to act as judge in Christ's stead, and all would rise when he entered.

Christ as judge was a typical theme at this time, heralding doomsday on entrances like the west front of Wells Cathedral, and over untold numbers of chancel arches. But within a few decades, Christ would be portrayed in a totally different way at Lichfield, as the cathedral found a new and distinctive identity.

ABOVE LEFT
The dean's seat features busts of Mary and Christ used as label-stops at the base of its surmounting arch.

ABOVE RIGHT
The northern capital of the dean's seat; the sculpture here is in comparatively good condition, vivid with symbolism.

LICHFIELD'S ROSES

Amongst the medieval carvings of Lichfield Cathedral, roses are prominent. This is neither accidental, nor merely decorative. The red and white roses were prominent symbols of the Virgin Mary, representing blood sacrifice and purity. The relationship was expressed through rosary beads, the earliest English reference to which comes from within this diocese in the mid-eleventh century, when Godgifu/Godiva of Coventry draped them as a gift over a statue of the Virgin at St Mary's Abbey, Coventry, which became Coventry Cathedral in 1102.

The western 'royal' portals at Notre-Dame, Chartres, of c.1145–55 feature a rose by the Virgin's shoulder. At Lichfield the double rose first features in the capitals flanking the dean's seat in the chapter house, in the mid-1240s. Lincoln Cathedral which, like Lichfield (in part), was dedicated to the Virgin Mary, presented sculpted roses in the Angel Choir (1256–80): that they were red can be seen from the surviving colour on the identical rose bosses of Bishop Remigius' contemporary tomb canopy. Lichfield's roses remained red in the late 1330s choir aisles. Those in the Lady Chapel arcades predate those in Ely's Lady Chapel, which was vaulted by the middle of the fourteenth century and where both red and white roses appear. With increasing consistency across Europe, artists depicted Mary as the Queen of Paradise surrounded by red and white rose bushes.

RIGHT
A late thirteenth-
century rose from
the 'Tomb of Christ'
at Lincoln Cathedral,
setting the context of
Christ's spilled blood
in a Marian cathedral.

OPPOSITE TOP LEFT
A red rose of c.1340
in the Marian church
of Lichfield.

OPPOSITE BOTTOM
LEFT
James Denton's
combined flower
from 1520, usually
called 'Tudor' but
actually a continental
form of Marian flower
that united the roses
of charity and chastity
in the 1470s, a device
adopted by Henry VII.

The rose bosses of Lichfield's north transept of the 1350s remained red, but one fifteenth-century exception is peculiarly interesting. In 1445 the cathedral had two fonts of silver gilt, 'having white roses in the middle and pounced with rays of the sun' six years before what we call the 'sun in splendour' was adopted as the heraldic device of Edward IV.[45] The combination symbolized a Marian purity in the creation of her 'son' – and Edward's choice of the symbol was to counter rumours spread of his bastardy, casting aspersions on his mother Cecily Neville, the 'Rose of Raby'.

The esteem of the rose grew further, flowering at Lichfield most spectacularly in the early sixteenth-century vault beneath the southwest tower. Its new patron was James Denton, Henry VIII's chaplain, dean of Lichfield 1522–33. We have habitually called this device the Tudor rose, reflecting the belief that fifteenth-century English monarchs had adopted the red rose (Lancaster) and the white rose (York) as dynastic symbols, which were then merged to represent blended Tudor blood – but this is incorrect. Before the early Tudor age many permutations of double white and red rose were specifically Marian, symbolizing through the two roses of paradise her righteous governance. In turn they represented monarchs as divinely-appointed 'types' of Christ and Mary, thus returning a country to the heavenly state promised in the book of Revelation. The famous ship charged with defending this island paradise, the *Mary Rose*, carried a symbol on its prow cut from the same stem as James Denton's bloom.

BELOW
Separate red and white roses, representing charity and chastity, in the Lady Chapel, Ely, from the same period as Lichfield's red roses.

The Nave

As Lichfield's chapter house progressed, Henry III was in the throes of turning Westminster into a new powerhouse of dynastic and biblical art, synthesizing the arts of France and Rome. It resembled the interior of Reims Cathedral, the French coronation church, but its details owed as much to the reliquary chapel of Henry's brother-in-law Louis IX, the Sainte-Chapelle.

Imperial overtones were quite the thing in the 1240s. Many marvelled at reports of a magnificent new two-storeyed chapel, the Sainte-Chapelle, in the royal palace of Paris, including Henry III of England, who had given building timber to Lichfield. Louis IX of France became St Louis; his piety was most conspicuously displayed through the Sainte-Chapelle, begun sometime after 1237 and consecrated on 16 April 1248. Its purpose was to house important relics of Christ and the Virgin, bought at vast expense from the last Latin emperor of Constantinople, Baldwin II (1228–73). The lower storey was dedicated to the Virgin Mary and held holy relics of her milk and hair. It remains lit by windows of a peculiar type – flattened convex triangles, sometimes inaptly called 'spherical triangles'.

ABOVE
Lichfield's nave, looking west; the modern banners may well give a sense of short-lived medieval dressings.

LEFT
Westminster Abbey, viewed through the crossing to the north transept. The royal adoption of Rheims-style 'bar tracery' here after 1245 spread to Lincoln, Hereford and Lichfield in the 1250s.

LEFT
Sainte-Chapelle,
Paris (after 1238),
the shrine-chapel
of Louis IX.
This astonishing
achievement
of structural
engineering and
applied arts inspired
key examples of
English court
architecture over
the next century.

BELOW
The undercroft
in the Sainte-
Chapelle, dedicated
to the Virgin, with
triangular windows in
the lateral walls which
provided the model
for Lichfield.

The upper principal level is a spectacular tall cage of largely original glass in vivid colours, showing a narrative cycle from Christ's infancy, in the north, to the Passion, in the east, then the life of St John the Evangelist (south). Sculpted figures of the 12 apostles punctuate the main supports, interrupting wall-shafts patterned with (restored) paint and gilding, while enamel and glass details in the lower arcade enliven the censing angels in the spandrels. The king and queen occupied cells recessed in the wall at the centre of the chapel. Here, they adored the contents of a gold reliquary, including what were believed to be a piece of the true cross, and the crown of thorns.

The French joked that Henry III, who saw it in 1254, would like to put it on a cart and lug it to London. He had already paraphrased aspects of the chapel's design at Westminster Abbey, begun in 1245. The abbey had several functions – it was the English coronation church and also a mausoleum, where the English kings could be appropriately buried in their capital city, rather than in various churches in northern France, or, like Henry's father, in Worcester. Henry employed censing angels in the spandrels high up in Westminster's transepts, and simplified versions of the convex triangle windows appear in the upper chambers of the ambulatory chapels. He also emulated Louis IX in purchasing a relic of the blood of Christ, delivered in a crystal phial in 1247.

Even before it was consecrated, the Sainte-Chapelle was a sensation, its relics coveted, its architecture emulated.

ABOVE

The nave exterior
from the south-east;
the lower window
arches carry three
even circles within a
convex triangle that
recall those in the
nave of Westminster
Abbey – but Lichfield
was built first.

In 1292 St Stephen's Chapel in Westminster was begun, as a delayed response to this Parisian royal chapel, being a two-storey glazed cage in England's principal royal palace. But Lichfield Cathedral, a Marian church with its own important collection of relics, and which was largely constructed in the century after 1250, remains much less recognized as an outstanding English tribute to this French architectural paragon.

Henry III's interest in Lichfield Cathedral, and his emulation at Windsor of what he had helped to achieve here, brought the cathedral into the consciousness of this great royal builder. It is true that the king similarly assisted other cathedrals, such as Wells. It is also true that his French minister, Bishop Aigueblanche of Hereford, built the north transept of his cathedral in close emulation of Westminster in around 1257. But it was Lichfield that most fully entered the circle of court architecture, establishing an evolving dialogue with royal works that clearly paraphrased London and Paris in Staffordshire.

It is tantalizing that the next iteration of an octagonal palm-vaulted chapter house was at Westminster Abbey. The event that may have turned Henry III's patronage of Lichfield into a concerted manifesto of court style was the battle of Bryn Derwin in June 1255, when Llewelyn ap Gruffudd (Llewelyn the Last), whose court was in Snowdonia, trounced his rivals Owain and Dafydd, to expand his territory eastward. Llewelyn then

became prince of all Gwynedd, a power in north Wales that soon threatened English interests in the north-eastern territory of Perfeddwlad (middle land). This led to the battle of Cadfan in 1257, when an English army led by Stephen Bauzan was shockingly defeated. Lichfield occupied the closest English diocese to the turmoil in north Wales, with Hereford to the south, and the architecture of both cathedrals began to express Henry III's Anglo-French royal interests.

It can be no coincidence that the first of the builders in the court style at Lichfield was the king's own cousin, Bishop Roger de Meyland. He was a canon of Lichfield, and was elevated as bishop of Coventry and Lichfield in the crucial year 1257. By this time Westminster Abbey had been 12 years in the making, and Lichfield's eight-bay nave began to be redeveloped as the clearest parallel to its language. But these comparisons are insufficient to suggest that the royal builders downed tools at Westminster and left for Lichfield. Instead, the masons' handiwork is closer to another great project, the Angel Choir of Lincoln Cathedral (1256–80). When Dean Mancetter died and was walled up in the Head Chapel Tower in 1254, he was replaced by Dean Ralph of Sempringham, a Lincolnshire name, whereupon bishop and dean brought Westminster and Lincoln together, fusing aspects of their two great buildings at Lichfield.

ABOVE

Lincoln Cathedral's Angel Choir, 1256–80, seen beyond the high altar; an outstanding evocation of a Marian paradise, with the angels acting as intercessors between depictions of the fall of man and Mary and Christ. It was built a year after the murder of a boy, Little St Hugh, which was blamed on Lincoln's Jews; his apparent martyrdom brought pilgrim traffic.

ABOVE
The elevation of Lichfield's Angel Choir, with trefoils in the main arcade spandrels and paired lights above in the triforium.

RIGHT
Lichfield's designer reinterpreted the design of the Angel Choir and added the convex triangular windows to form a clerestory.

The masons of Lichfield's nave were spared one headache; the main arcade has no fashionable hard dark marble shafts, as at Westminster and Lincoln (and Canterbury, Salisbury and others), since their building harmonized with the old choir. But the carved decoration reveals the hand of the Lincoln workshop. The fighting dragons of the nave aisle vault bosses compare precisely with those on Lincoln's Angel Choir portals.

Lichfield's nave arcades have complex arches, and the outer mouldings terminate with expressive heads of superb quality.[46] In the early thirteenth century, great church architecture emulated shrines, with projecting heads, quatrefoils, gabled canopies and other applied features of the metalwork of gilded reliquaries that contained hallowed remains.[47] At Lincoln after 1256 we find applied trefoils, suggestive of magnified metal wire decoration. Lichfield similarly shows circles in the spandrels between the nave arcade arches enclosing cinquefoils. Above these are quatrefoils in the tracery of the triforium's paired windows, evoking Westminster's fresh tracery, and then trefoils in the three circles of the clerestory windows within convex triangles. Presenting five, four and then three cusps in ascending order asserts a rational sequence, but it may also have held numerological associations with biblical themes.[48]

The convex triangle windows follow the wall-ribs of the vault, a brilliant solution matching Sainte-Chapelle's lower chapel, being a variation on its tripartite cusped tracery. Why is Lichfield as comparable to Sainte-Chapelle as to Westminster? If Westminster and Lichfield both refer to the French model, then the language of Lichfield's nave coalesces into an essay on three of the great shrine churches of its age: the English royal abbey dedicated to St Peter, the Marian element of Sainte-Chapelle, and the shrine church erected around the tomb of St Hugh of Lincoln that evoked a Marian paradise. Lichfield's ancient origins would have been well served by these associations, a metropolitan authority to underpin the royal campaign in Wales.[49]

The nave awkwardly negotiates the thickness of the western towers, suggesting their cores pre-existed. The running moulding – more a magnified cumin-seed than the usual

ABOVE LEFT
Lichfield's nave features fearsome dragons, symbols of evil, biting at each others' throats in hopeless bloodlust.

ABOVE RIGHT
Lincoln's choir portals carry slain dragons of extremely similar form – so similar as to suggest they were carved by the same hands as Lichfield.

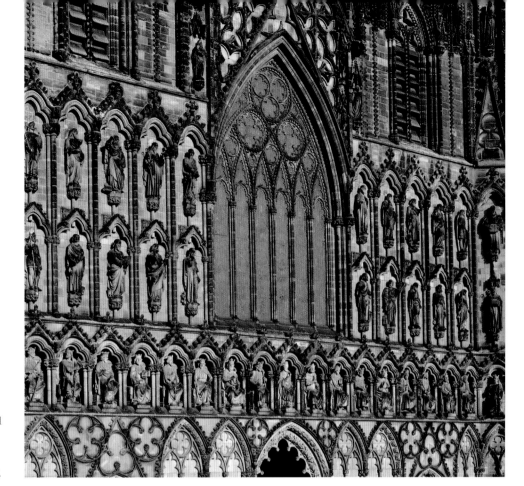

RIGHT
Lichfield's west front
features 113 figures,
only five of which
are medieval. The
west window is an
inauthentic design
of George Gilbert
Scott's, dating to
c.1869, which replaced
another inauthentic
wheel window from
the reign of Charles II.

pyramidal dogtooth – mitigates this by asserting a unifying sculptural treatment. The bosses generally represent leaves or fighting and bestial behaviour in the lower arcades, elevated to the coronation of the Virgin in the easternmost high vault boss. Another original boss remains in the choir, a mutilated Annunciation, but the central bays were rebuilt from 1789.

The west front is a screen façade, perhaps the last of the great billboards of English façade sculpture. Beyond its ornamental impact, this type of façade evoked the mansions of heaven. That it does not extend beyond the width of the nave, unlike other examples, could be another symptom of retained Norman towers. The nave's cinquefoil circles were carried through to the lowest level of the exterior, where a Christ in Majesty surrounded by instruments of the Passion still amazingly survives above the central door. The Church, as *Ecclesia*, was one of Mary's personifications, as shown in Lincoln's Judgement Portal, the pilgrims' entrance to its Angel Choir. At Lichfield she was perhaps always represented by the (since restored) central column-figure beneath Christ.[50] Through this portal, bishops represented Christ's spiritual presence in processions, passing by the iron door-hinges made by Thomas Leighton in 1293.

One of their number was buried under a similar arch by the other main entrance, the south wall of the transept. His effigy clutches a book. Who was this biblical scholar? He remains anonymous, a tantalizing challenge. And what was his understanding of Lichfield Cathedral? Perhaps we can get closer to the latter question.

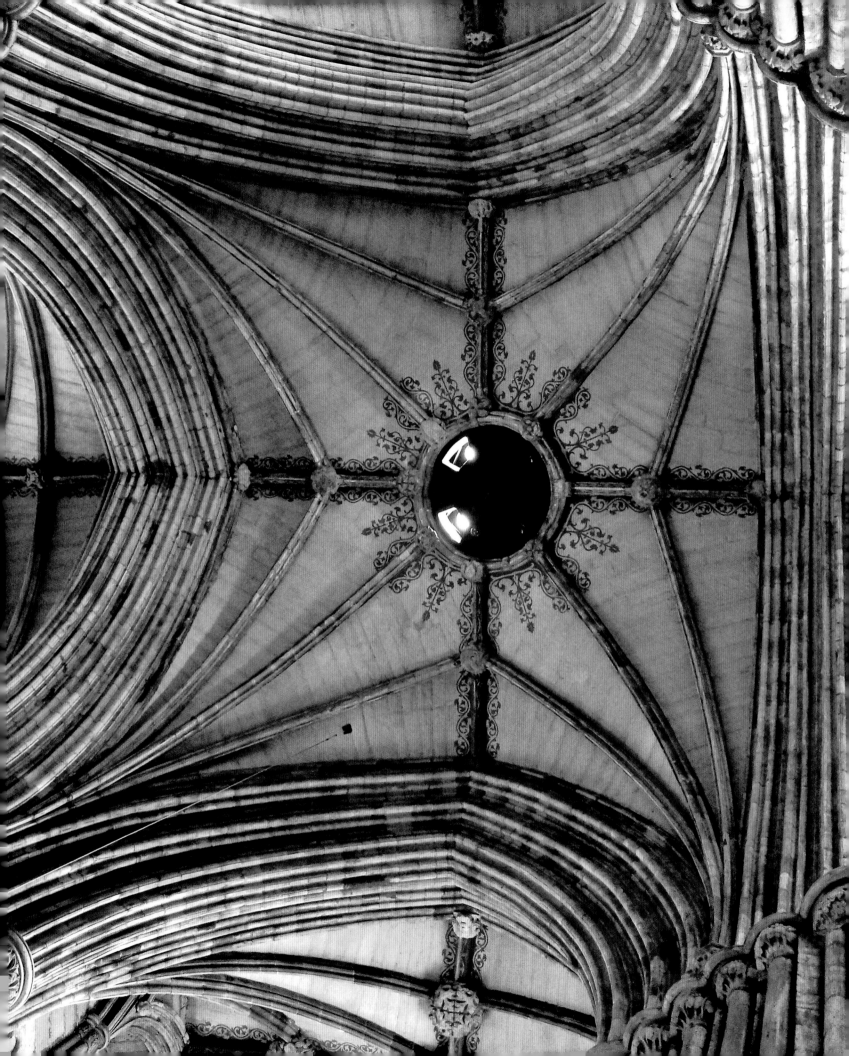

OPPOSITE
The crossing and
transepts played an
important role as a
fitting threshold to
the rebuilt east end,
which included the
feretory containing
Chad's main shrine.

BELOW RIGHT
Wells Cathedral's
moated close,
containing the
castellar hall built
by Bishop Robert
Burnell (1275–92),
with a later moat and
curtain wall of c.1330.

PREVIOUS SPREAD
The south transept
vault was inserted
in the early 1350s,
just after the Black
Death, the resulting
shortage of workmen
probably explaining
the charmingly
overblown scale
and crudeness of its
details in comparison
with the refined
choir. Replacing
taller timber vaults a
century old, the new
vaults apparently
offered a brace for
the heavy stone spire,
then rising over the
central crossing.

3

Exploring the Shrine Church, 1300–1538

In the 1290s, the vast effort of building Edward I's Welsh Castles was marshalled through Chester, in the diocese of Coventry and Lichfield. But the city of Lichfield itself needed reconstruction after a great fire in 1291. Those who ventured to its cloth and leather markets or popular fairs would have encountered a vast building site, the 'ladder streets' echoing from mallets beating pegs into oak beams. Across the water of Minster Pool, the cathedral close was unaffected by the flames. The great church was now approaching completion, with a renewed commitment to court arts. In the cathedral sacristy were six gold morses – clasps for securing prelates' robes – each studded with precious stones. These were the gifts of Henry III and Edward I, literal badges of honour, but in the decades before the Black Death of 1349–53 the direct royal favour shown to Lichfield was far outweighed by the munificence of its courtier-bishops. The greatest of these were Walter Langton and Roger de Northburgh.

On 19 February 1296 the chapter elected Walter Langton as bishop. He was born Walter Peverel, at Thorpe Langton in Leicestershire; the fortunes of the Peverel family, once richly rewarded by William the Conqueror, had declined since William Peverel lost the favour of Henry II (1154–89) amidst charges of witchcraft and the poisoning of the earl of Chester.[51] Starting his career at York Minster, where his uncle was dean, Walter was to follow in the wake of Robert Burnell, archdeacon of York, bishop of Bath and Wells, treasurer of England, counselor to Edward I (1272–1307) and great builder of castellar palaces at Wells and Acton Burnell, Shropshire.

Langton replaced Burnell as the king's chief minister through his career as a clerk of the king's wardrobe from 1290 and his promotion to keeper of the wardrobe, a trusted role managing the intricacies of court decorum. King Edward led one of the great building campaigns of medieval Europe, the new castles in the territories he had conquered in north Wales, and the marshalling-point for this vast effort was Chester, within the Coventry and Lichfield diocese.

Edward I inherited his father Henry III's incomplete but exceptionally rich work at Westminster Abbey, which galvanized the sacred presentation of the English monarchy. In 1272 Henry was buried in a marble tomb, probably over a supposed relic of Christ's blood. His superb bronze effigy remains, plated in Florentine gold, parallelling the shrine of the Saxon saint and king, Edward the Confessor. Work was still unfinished when Edward acceded.

By the time Langton became royal treasurer in 1295, he was also a canon of Lichfield. As both Edward's chief minister, and bishop from 1296, he mixed royal service with ministry at Lichfield's altar. It would be surprising if, in his 25 years of journeying between London and Lichfield, Langton did not import some of the cosmopolitan Westminster style into Staffordshire.

OPPOSITE
The surviving north-east tower of the Bishop's Palace is polygonal, like the Eagle Tower at Edward I's Caernarvon Castle, an imperial mode that was in turn inspired by Roman Constantinople.

BELOW LEFT
Plan of the Bishop's Palace, destroyed during the Civil War. Much remains unclear about its evolution, but the Great Hall contained murals of Edward I.

The Bishop's Palace

LANGTON'S EXPERIENCE OF ROYAL BUILDING AND IMAGERY WAS ONLY HALF THE story. This was also an age of grand bishops' palaces. To the north of Westminster Abbey's royal portal, Langton would have known York Place as the seat of the archbishops of York, recently established by Archbishop Walter de Grey (it became 'Whitehall' after 1530).[52] Langton built a turreted residence for Coventry and Lichfield near Temple Bar, the licence to crenellate dated 19 June 1305.[53] The parish chosen was 'St Mary atte Stronde'.

At Lichfield, Langton rebuilt the palace to the east of his cathedral to a royal scale and style. Its walls were up to 16 m (52 ft) high, with polygonal turrets evoking Constantinople's immense turreted walls – a famous vision of imperial glory known to crusaders, including King Edward himself, whose architect was building similar turrets topped with eagles for the Prince of Wales' lodgings at Caernarvon Castle. In short, Langton conjured an Edwardian palace in Lichfield cathedral close, overlooking Stowe Pool and Chad's oratory. In the 1590s, half a century before the palace was wrecked in the Civil War, the county historian Sampson Erdeswick described Langton's

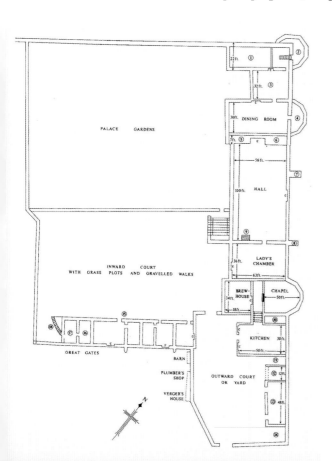

enormous hall of 30 x 17 m (100 x 56 ft), an area larger than the Great Hall of Hampton Court, as presenting a magnificent first impression to visitors:

> A goodly large hall, wherein hath been excellently well painted, but now much decayed, the coronation, marriage, wars, and funeral of Edward I; and some writing, where there is also yet remaining which expresseth the meaning of the history: where is especially mentioned the behaviour of Sir Roger Pewlesdon, and others, against the Welshmen; as also of Almaric de Bailgiol, Burnell, Valence earl of Pembroke, of the lord Badlesmere, and other barons, against the Scots where the said earls and lords are very lively portrayed, with their banners of arms bravely before them.

One might ask whether any religious imagery lurked amongst these themes of royal prerogative and violence; yet righteousness was implicit. The scheme echoes the Painted Chamber, inner sanctum of Westminster Palace. Henry III's murals of c.1263 showed, as the principal focus behind the royal bedstead, the coronation of St Edward the Confessor, the seated king flanked by bishops[54]. The surrounding walls featured additional pictures of c.1292, which Langton must have seen freshly painted. They portrayed the righteous militancy of the Old Testament kings and the fate of tyrants, while the raking window jambs showed virtues trampling vices. Militarism and its arts counted for much in the age of crusades and territorial expansion, when God was assumed to be on the side of the victor. The bishop of Coventry and Lichfield was a linchpin in this culture, his palace set half-way between Westminster and Caernarvon.

Langton didn't stop there. He rebuilt yet another palace, the moated Eccleshall Castle, as the bishops' country seat, and a crenellated hunting residence at Beaudesert

BELOW

The Lady Chapel
from the north-east;
before the choir was
built up to it after
1337, its free-standing
form more closely
resembled the Sainte-
Chapelle. Note how
this extension was
built over falling
ground, which was
avoided by the shorter
Norman church.

Hall. In 1299 he surpassed even the moated, walled palace of Wells, fortifying Lichfield's entire cathedral close by a ring of walls with defensible towers, quite the *hortus conclusus*. Langton's own statue was set in the north-west tower, and the remains of the south-eastern gate can still be seen from Dam Street.

Largesse often comes at a price; the bishop's promotions and wealth certainly brought him trouble, against which the king's protection proved to be of limited comfort. The Lincoln Parliament of 1301 attempted to unseat Langton, although Edward I stepped in; but when the king died in 1307, his son Edward II and his favourite Piers Gaveston took against Lichfield's bishop. Langton had to venture to Rome to seek papal absolution against spectacular charges by Sir John Lovetot, including not only adultery (with Lovetot's stepmother), but the murder of the plaintiff's father. Charges of devil-worshipping, simony, and pluralism followed; quite the royal flush of accusations, each an echo of the Peverel family's old reputation. Langton never fully recovered. The dean and chapter of Lichfield defended their bishop from these 'slanders' – but it is telling that they did so on the grounds of his architectural achievements. These were investments in redemption.

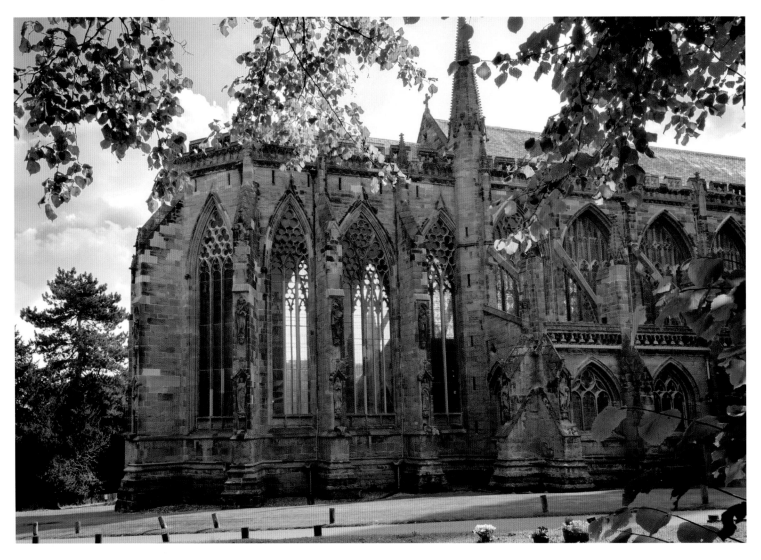

Langton:
The Lady Chapel and Cathedral Furnishings

————

BEYOND BUILDING HIS PALACES AND RAISING THE DEFENCES OF THE CLOSE, Langton had unfinished business in the cathedral itself. He paid the astonishing sum of £2,000 for a suitable replacement for St Chad's shrine, a gabled form made of gold and jewels in Paris. It was now far removed from the simple and elegant painted stonework of the Lichfield Angel, half a millennium earlier, and must have borne comparison with Becket's main shrine at Canterbury, with a similar function as the principal one among four separate shrines.[55] Matthew Paris explained that such caskets were inevitably inferior to the relics they contained, the latter being 'more precious than gold and precious jewels.'[56] We can only imagine its effect in candlelight, bound by a feretory of timber and iron screens.

Langton contributed much besides: altar cloths, a pyx for the body of Christ at the Eastertide procession, a jeweled chalice worth £80, and tunics and rich copes. The most spectacular was a gold standing altar cross, displaying not only jewels but what was believed to be a relic of Christ's crucifix:

> Also one noble cross of pure gold with a noble foot of pure gold, of the value of two hundred pounds, the gift of Walter de Langedon, Bishop, everywhere ornamented with precious stones; in which the image of the crucified is fixed on one side, while over the other is impressed one small cross of the wood of our Lord's cross, as is believed; upon the other side are fixed diverse stones precious and of great value, namely, six rubies, five sapphires, fifteen larger emeralds ('and one is wanting'), and one broken, besides smaller ones; sixteen large pearls, beside innumerable small ones.[57]

By way of comparison, Langton's lavishness rather outshone the builder of the nave: 'two small portable crosses, one of which is covered with silver plates, and the other copper gilt, the gift of Roger de Meuland.'

Langton donated many of these pieces for display in the cathedral's century-old choir, and no doubt others were to furnish his astonishing new Lady Chapel, begun around 1310–15, probably to the designs of William de Eyton. This is based on interior plan dimensions of 16.5 x 8 m (54 x 27 ft), a double-square proportion also followed in Ely Cathedral's Lady Chapel.[58] It has long been admired, a tall and elegant volume that complemented the vaulting of the chapter house and nave. Its windows now host Renaissance glass (see Appendix) but in the fourteenth century the colours were likely to have combined some of the newly-contrived straw-yellow washes of silver nitrate with grey-white and deeper shades of green, blue, and red. The crucifixion almost certainly featured in the east window, as was customary.

OPPOSITE
The interior of the
Lady Chapel, shown
while the Herkenrode
glass was removed
for conservation.
The plain glass gives
a sense of the quality
of the lighting that
would have been
experienced between
the Civil War and late
eighteenth century.

It is of singular interest that the jewelled gold cross Langton gave held a relic of the wood of Christ's cross ('as was believed'), directly comparable to another fragment venerated in the Sainte-Chapelle. We have seen how Lichfield's nave employed the convex triangle window type of the Sainte-Chapelle's Marian lower chapel in tandem with Lincoln's features, but the Lady Chapel represents a much more literal reflection of the main body of the Sainte-Chapelle. The windows in the polygonal apses are stacks of trefoils in both cases, the broader side windows similarly elaborated with a round oculus. Perhaps the most striking comparison is that between the Sainte-Chapelle's 12 apostles, standing within the wall-shafts so that they become 'pillars of the church'. There are 10 such niches at Lichfield, lined with red and green medieval paint and now occupied by Victorian replacement statues, but if the since-removed western return wall once held two other niches in a regular spacing, there would have been the full complement of a dozen. Finally, the Sainte-Chapelle had low booths for the king and queen, as recesses within the arcading, akin to the exceptional arrangement of the Lichfield Lady Chapel's distinctive southern funerary chapel.

BELOW LEFT
The Lady Chapel with
Herkenrode glass
and accompanying
panel to the right
(the south-west).

BELOW RIGHT
The Lady Chapel
vault, part of an
unusually harmonic
ensemble of vaults
from the nave to the
transepts. spanning
a hundred years.

LEFT
The Victorian
restored figures
are set within an
arrangement of
niches incorporated
into the wall-shafts
as a direct inspiration
from the Sainte-
Chapelle.

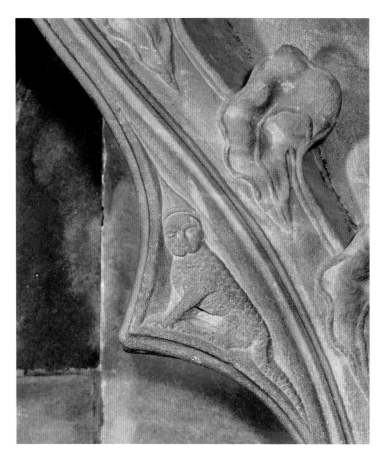 

ABOVE

Rich architectural detailing further enhances Langton's ambitious Lady Chapel.

All this represents the highest of ambitions – royal Paris in Staffordshire – yet the building was left unfinished by Langton, who may have planned to be buried in the side chapel within sight of the altar. Also incomplete was the far western end of the cathedral, where the screen façade's pink stones were being freshly cut. Their courses rose gradually into tiered arcades framing statues of kings and saints, above the richest of English cathedral doors. When Langton expired in the dead of winter in February 1321, the cathedral needed new energy, another champion.

Roger de Northburgh

ROGER DE NORTHBURGH, BISHOP OF LICHFIELD 1321–58, SHOULD BE BETTER known. He amply filled Langton's episcopal slippers and contributed a tremendous architectural legacy at this cathedral and far beyond.

Like Langton, he took a toponym, hailing from Northborough, a small village on the edge of the Fens in the soke of Peterborough (now Cambridgeshire). Also like his predecessor, Roger was a clerk of the royal wardrobe, and the storerooms of Edward II were very rich indeed, though unaccountably funded, a situation that Northburgh helped to reform in 1318. His licence for election as bishop was granted 13 days after Langton's

NORTHBOROUGH MANOR

Bishop Northburgh had aspirations far beyond his birthplace but it seems that the his allegiance to his homeland remained strong, as he appointed Ralph of Holbeach (near Spalding) as his deputy and made John of Depyng (Market Deeping, one mile north of Northborough) the chancellor of Lichfield in 1329.[59]

He brought his ambitions home by building a substantial house in fine limestone, one of the best survivors of its age.[60] Between 1333 and 1336, the bishop constructed a gatehouse, leading to a new residence with a great hall at its centre. This house substantially survives, its eastern staircase well once leading to the solar block which contained the bishop's bedchamber. The western gable features chunky crockets like a procession of tortoises. Where did he find his inspiration? It might offer us a hint of the character of the lost episcopal palace at Lichfield.

death, amidst a dispute with Coventry, and without help from Edward II. But the king depended on Northburgh, who brought with him to Lichfield William Harlaston, a royal clerk who was entrusted with the great seal. In this age of papal schism, numerous posts were filled by absenteeists appointed by the pope in Avignon, where Northburgh's own dean was in attendance, while many Italian clerics arrived in Lichfield.[61] This bishop was hands-on, his anxiety for progress creating friction with the chapter, though it assured momentum for Langton's unfinished architectural work.

When Langton's Lady Chapel was completed under Northburgh's watch, it stood somewhat isolated from the choir, similar to the arrangement at Hereford, where the Lady Chapel is linked to the church by an eastern 'ambulatory' aisle. It would not remain so for long.

In the 1330s, the pressing task was to remodel the choir, and for this Bishop Northburgh sought the counsel of William Ramsey III, one of the principal English architects of the later Middle Ages. Ramsey cultivated the Perpendicular style, named for its relentless verticality of window mullions and applied stone panelling, presenting a unified grid that speaks of order. By 1332 he was busy at St Paul's Cathedral, masterminding the highly original two-storey octagonal chapter house, uniquely placed in the centre of the cloisters.[62] As a royal surveyor, Ramsey was an obvious choice for an episcopal servant for Edward II, who had inherited Langton's lofty ambition. It is here in the choir that Lichfield's late medieval identity became crystallized.

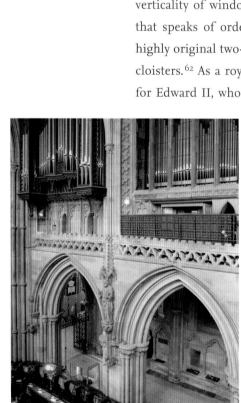

Whether by direction or at his own suggestion, William Ramsey unified the Lady Chapel with the choir and sanctuary after 1337, making advisory visits from London. The old choir was levelled, leaving just the three westernmost arches of the main arcades to prop the crossing tower, together with the treasury and Head Chapel Tower to the south and the chapter house and its vestibule opposite. To that rump, Ramsey added an eastward extension of the main arcade, with cinquefoils that clearly relate to those in the nave and on the west front: a remarkable approach to uniformity that is hard to parallel. This is topped by a uniform clerestory of large windows lined with fashionable chamfered jambs of quatrefoils.[63] The result is a two-storey elevation in harmony with the Lady Chapel and the transepts, a model of modern elegance.

LEFT
View into the choir through Skidmore's Victorian iron screen. The medieval pulpitum would typically have been made of stone, with only a narrow view through a central portal.

BELOW LEFT
The two bays retained from the choir built in the last years of the twelfth century, abutting the tower. The structural value arising from their position may have been instrumental in their retention.

OPPOSITE
The choir from the east. Here, we can appreciate the two-storey system that unites the new choir with the transepts, and the bisected cinquefoils that continue the theme of the nave and west front.

The (restored) canopied wall-shaft niches with statues set over the choir stalls followed the Lady Chapel's examples. Thomas Pennant recorded the figures in their damaged state, confirming that the subjects were correctly restored in the Victorian era:

> On each side are six statues, now much mutilated, placed in beautiful gothic niches, and richly painted. The first on the left is St. *Peter*; the next is the Virgin; the third is *Mary Magdalene*, with one leg bare, to denote her legendary wantonness. The other three are St. *Philip*, St. *James*, and St. *Christopher*, with CHRIST on his shoulders.

The relationship between them is martyrdom; all made a blood sacrifice, being either crucified or beheaded, or were integral to Christ's crucifixion. The choice of these figures would have greatly heightened the drama of the Mass in this new choir, when the focus of Lichfield's canons at the elevation of the host would be the supposed fragment of the

THE LICHFIELD SACRIST'S ROLL

This list of relics was recorded by sacrist Dan Richard Mareschall in 1345. Though many of the objects appear to have been kept in storage in the sacristy, the positions of shrines reveal something of the geography of the cathedral in Roger de Northburgh's time, but with many objects given by Walter Langton.

> In the first place the head of Blessed Chad in a certain painted wooden case. Also an arm of Blessed Chad. Also bones of the said saint in a certain portable shrine. Also two silver shrines beyond the High Altar with the relics of divers saints. Also the great shrine of Saint Chad, of the value of two thousand pounds, the gift of Walter, Bishop. Also ten coffers with the relics of diverse saints sealed with diverse seals. And part of the wood which the Lord planted and it is called Coket. Also some of the bones of S. Laurence. Some of the Mount Calvary. Some of Golgotha. Some of the dust of St Amphibalus. A piece of the rock standing upon which Jesus wept bitterly and wept over Jerusalem. Some of the bones of the eleven Thousand Virgins. Part of the sepulcher of the Blessed Virgin. Some (relics) of the Innocents. (A relic) of S. Wolfad. Part of the finger and cowl of S. William. Part of the mitre of S. Anselm. Part of the cross and of the sepulcher of S. Andrew. Some sardine oil [mistranslated; this is a relic of oil from a painted image of the virgin at Saidnaya, Syria].[64] Some of the bones of S. Stephen. Some of the bones of S. Helen. Some of the bread of S. Godric. Part of the haubergeon of S. Godric. Some of the bones of S. James. Some of the blood and of the napkin of S. Gereon, Bishop of Cologne. Some of the wood of the cross of S. Peter. Some of the bones of S. Barbara. Part of the sepulcher of our Lord. Part of the hair shirt of S. Cuthbert. Part of a garment of S. Saturninus. Part of the tomb of S. Laurence and or his gridiron. Part of the head of S. Blase. Part of the arm of S. Symeon.

crucifix set within Bishop Langton's glittering altar cross, a physical witness and proof of Christ's suffering to set before the celebrants, amongst relics of the suffering of other martyrs.[65]

Over the celebrants' heads stood these exalted martyrs – described as gilded in 1634 – and supported by angels as intercessors between heaven and earth. In this context, the cinquefoils may have recalled the five wounds of Christ.[66] To cement the point, Mary's red rose of sacrifice forms the boss that locks the stone vault of the north aisle behind her. This poses perhaps the most important question relating to the cathedral's medieval identity; why was this theme of martyrdom and blood sacrifice chosen? After all, St Chad was not martyred.

The answer appears to lie in a mid-thirteenth-century search for the etymology of 'Lichfield', wrongly believed to mean 'Field of the corpses'.[67] A myth was then promoted by Matthew Paris of St Albans Abbey, claiming that Lichfield saw the slaughter of 999 Christian martyrs from Verulamium (Roman St Albans) under Diocletian (284–305). They had been converted by (the invented) St Amphibalus, and at Lichfield were restored bodily and sent to heaven by his intercession. John Lydgate represented a fifteenth-century understanding of the 'euerlasting gladness in that place […] where ioie folwith of euerlastyng liff':[68]

ABOVE
Daniel King's engraving shows the gable of the west front prior to Civil War damage and the removal to Swynnerton of the 2-metre-high seated Christ in the gable apex. This early-fourteenth-century Christ points to the wound made by Longinus' spear, from which his martyrial blood spilled.

> Bi the prayer of Amphibauls
>
> Off ded bodyes with their woundis greene,
>
> A gret miracle, the story tellith thus,
>
> Ther woundis hol that no carect was seene,
>
> Ioyned togidre & sowdid eke so cleene;
>
> A strunge siht, a siht of gret delite,
>
> The blody strem as mylk ran don al white.
>
> […]
>
> For vnto god nothing is impossible,
>
> For their that wer manglid & deformyd,
>
> Bi grace & praier wer sodenly reformyd
>
> John Lydgate *The Life of St Alban and St Amphibal*
> (lines 3691–3704)

Lichfield's lasting association with this myth led to the uncomfortable choice of limbs and corpses for the city's coat of arms after 1549, while the motto 'The Church is the seed of the blood of the Martyrs' translates one of the Latin lines inscribed in the old parish church of St Mary.[69] But it has gone unnoticed that the cathedral represented the story on its own terms; blood sacrifice was central to the imagery of the completed west front. Above the west door, we have seen Christ seated with the instruments of the Passion, including the cross and crown of thorns. Then, around 1320, the central gable received another seated figure of Christ, which remarkably still survives at St Mary's Swynnerton

OPPOSITE
The north aisle
of the choir shows
the junction of the
surviving section of
the older choir with
William Ramsey's
remodelling,
where the vaults
have a ridge-rib.
The entrance to
the chapter house
vestibule on the left
also dates from the
earlier build.

ABOVE RIGHT
The city arms,
featuring corpses and
severed limbs, reflects
a myth of Christian
martyrdom linked
with Lichfield by the
chronicler Matthew
Paris.

RIGHT
The spandrels of the
arcades that once
led to the shrine
of St Chad features
angels' heads and
wings (the furthest
is a restoration).
Similar examples can
be seen in Lincoln's
eastern transepts
of c.1192, but they
became popular for
shrine-churches.
In Lichfield's case,
Chad's legend held a
special relationship
with visiting angels.

(26 miles north of Lichfield), where it is far too large for its situation.[70] It is covered in traces of medieval colour and partly broken, suggestive of a rescue from Lichfield during the Civil War. Christ was the appropriate subject for this position beneath the gable's cross, and Daniel King's engraving confirms that the medieval sculpture had bent knees. Crucially, this particular figure of Christ is revealing the wound from Longinus' spear.[71]

These associations come just after Henry III's importation of the relic of Christ's blood to Westminster in 1247.[72] If Lichfield's bloody mythology were part of this cult, informing the west front's presentation of Christ as martyr, then Langton's fragment of the True Cross, the choir's martyrs, and the red roses of Marian blood sacrifice all augmented a powerfully focused narrative. The curiously militant imagery of the Bishop's Palace may also relate to personal blood sacrifice. In turn, all this explains Lichfield's insistent paraphrasing of Sainte-Chapelle, the most famous of all the repositories of blood relics.[73]

To return to the choir's aisles, along which the multitudes pursued this promise of everlasting life, the wall-arcade niches feature angels in their spandrels, set beneath bosses showing Chad's cross and the grapes symbolizing Christ's eucharistic blood. The angels looked toward St Chad's shrine, where more of their kind featured on the shrine base itself. Together they augmented Bede's account of how angels descended at Lichfield before Chad's death, but pilgrims now believed that Chad was not the first to be taken to heaven here; to them he had become witness to Lichfield's earlier role in delivering salvation for the common believer. No other English cathedral shared this dual identity; popular donations in its wake would account for the quality of building here, in a comparatively poor diocese, and the compulsion for royal support as a display of anti-tyrannical, pro-Christian virtue.

St Chad's arms held
by an angel on a vault
boss of the north
aisle, near the site
of his shrine.

The bosses in the high vaults of the choir have been damaged by exposure to rainwater, but they represent the Holy Trinity, the Assumption of the Virgin and the Coronation of the Virgin. Over St Chad's shrine is a boss showing monstrous fighting dragons, similar to those seen in the nave aisles and associated with brutality,[74] juxtaposed by another boss as a mass of gilded buttercups.[75] Beneath it, on one of Ramsey's northern piers, is a leafy buttercup capital from which a head emerges to look over the shrine. The consistency is striking, and explicable by comparison with the 'tomb of Christ' in Lincoln's Angel Choir, which uses this flower (with oak leaves) to speak of resurrection. A medieval name for the buttercup was 'Our Lady's bowl', from its resemblance to a golden chalice; here the eucharist blood is the theme. The whole ensemble tells us that the brutality of martyrdom, and the intercession of Mary and the Holy Trinity, can bring about salvation.

To make the idea literally tangible, the cathedral hosted among its relics the 'dust of St Amphibalus' and a clod of earth purportedly from Golgotha, stained from Christ's blood. The Virgin was a martyr through the sacrifice of her son, and what was heralded as a chunk of Mary's own sepulchre, probably brought back from a pilgrimage of a thousand miles and more, no doubt represented the earthly point of departure for her painless bodily assumption and subsequent coronation as Queen of Heaven.[76] We might expect these to have been displayed in the feretory and Lady Chapel.

The gallery projecting into the south choir aisle from the Head Chapel of St Chad was an integral part of the works to the choir, the suspended relic to be held aloft on principal feast days. All its relics enlivened the building, creating narratives and informing its planning. In the paths of these saints and martyrs, the afflicted, fearful and hopeful sought to follow.

The bosses in the choir vault showing, left to right: the Coronation of the Virgin, perhaps abstracted buttercup leaves; medieval leaf forms speaking of the Christian concept of rebirth into the eternal spring of Paradise; and the Assumption of the Virgin, with Mary in a vesica carried aloft by angels. Tendrils and leaves lie overhead.

The late-thirteenth-century Christ's tomb at Lincoln; buttercups like golden chalices and oak leaves sprout from an implicit acorn, combining to represent Christ's blood generating robust new life.

Remodelling the Transepts

THE IDIOSYNCRATIC MEDIEVAL TRANSEPT VAULTS HAVE EVADED FIRM attribution.[77] Their big bosses hang like so many great chrysanthemums, pinning the junctions of ribs that are spanned by stone slabs the size of coffin lids. Everything seems over-scaled, and this pattern of vaulting became old-fashioned during the fourteenth century, abandoned in favour of net-like complexities. So when did these vaults replace the timber ceiling that Henry III admired, and why? A clue to their date can be found in the capitals of the extended wall-shafts, featuring small crenellations that belong to the fourteenth and fifteenth centuries. A still closer inspection confirms that the transept remodelling dates to the ebb of the plague known as the Black Death, which struck in 1348. It is related to a letter written by Bishop Northburgh early in 1352 to explain that the dean and chapter, 'newly setting to work, are trying, with God's help and at great expense, to restore modern elegance (*ad novitatis decorem*) to the work that pious antiquity built in its own style (*suo more*).'[78]

Transforming the transepts would certainly have involved great expense. But the shape of the vaults, with five ribs meeting at the ridge in each bay, was merely a continuation of those built with finer bosses in William Ramsey's choir, which in turn followed the pattern

of *c.*1315 in the Lady Chapel, itself not dissimilar to the thirteenth-century nave. Hence the conservative style was a sustained attempt at harmonizing all the high vaults.[79]

It is telling that the transepts' clerestory window tracery is comparable to that of the choir, but the clearest indication that some of the masons building the choir continued their work into the transepts is the design of the ridge ribs (along and across the apexes of the vault), which closely replicate the wavy tendril and flower pattern of those in the choir vaults. The transepts' wall surfaces are clad with stone framing reminiscent of recent work on the transepts of Gloucester Cathedral, and the style of the bearded faces with curled bouffant hair on bosses in the south transept further supports this date. The roughness of execution when compared to the choir suggests a dearth of talent amongst supervisors and masons after the ravages of the Black Death, among whose victims was William Ramsey himself, who died early in the summer of 1349. Small wonder that Northburgh depended on 'God's help' when two fifths of the populace were now buried in plague-pits.

The question of why the transepts were vaulted in stone in the midst of this turmoil begs a practical explanation, probably in the

LEFT
When the transepts were remodelled in 1352 the king was Edward III, who is the likeliest attribution for this bearded character. The second head may be Christ, or God the Father.

OPPOSITE
In the early 1350s, the transepts' thirteenth-century stiff-leaf capitals were crudely trimmed to make neat supports for the crenellated capitals supporting the new stone vault ribs.

OVERLEAF
The north transept vault, an irregular array of ribs linked by foliate bosses, which hint at the paradise looked up to by pilgrims and terminate to the north (right) with a magnificent Marian rose.

OPPOSITE

The cathedral seen
from the north-
west, showing the
completed spires. A
library once occupied
the space to the left
(north) of the nave;
a conduit head was
in the foreground.

shape of a tall stone spire being newly built on the adjacent crossing tower. Such massive weight requires bracing, as it will push against the transepts as much as against the stone-vaulted nave and choir. The old timber rib-and-plank vaults were no match for stone shells set in equilibrium. As the tower is accepted to be 'concurrent with the remodelling of the east end, and was designed by the same master', we can ascribe the first tall stone spire to these same years.[80]

In 1358 Northburgh followed Ramsay to the grave, probably buried beneath a chest monument set to the south of St Chad's shrine in the choir he had built. By then his work was done. With the completion of the choir, transepts, west front and the uneven west spires, the major building work was essentially finished. The remainder of the fourteenth and the fifteenth centuries may have seen new stained glass, but the cathedral had reached maturity as a shrine centre and a magnificent home for many tomb monuments, since lost.

One likely relic of Northburgh's own burial is a gold ring, found trampled by looters. Within 21 garnets is a face cut into chalcedony. Who this might be, looking back at us across the centuries, we can only guess.

ABOVE

An early-fourteenth-
century ring with a
head carved from
chalcedony, probably
a reused Roman
amulet of Medusa,
already a thousand
years old.

The Fifteenth Century

THE CATHEDRAL ONCE OWNED A COPE DECORATED WITH THE WHITE HART OF Richard II (1377–99), reminding us that donors presented furnishings and vestments well after the major building work had ended. This particular royal donor in 1387 licensed, and was patron of, a guild of St Mary and John the Baptist (another conspicuous blood martyr) in Lichfield, to which both clergy and citizens belonged.[81]

The completed cathedral was a house of 13 altars, filled with sculpted, engraved, painted and woven embellishments. Few traces of these remain. A major feature was the early fifteenth-century reredos, which once divided the altar from the feretory and St Chad's shrine with an array of saints, but was defaced by iconoclasts and pulled down by James Wyatt in the late 1780s. Another notable addition of the time is the mural painting of the assumption of the Virgin over the inside face of the chapter house door. Apparently paid for by Dean Heywood (1457–92), it shows the canons raising their hands in prayer as she is received by God, the necessary prelude to her coronation.[82] This was a subject dear

to Henry VI, who experienced the scene as a vision three times. The mural may even have been made with him in mind, as Henry VI showed particular favour after 1451 to this, the diocese of the Lancastrian heartlands. In St Mary's Guildhall, Coventry, there remains a stained glass window showing him among conquering kings and emperors – shoring up his reputation before the mayor and burghers, as his rule became threatened. He gave a blue mantle to St Michael's, Coventry, in 1451; he and the queen led theatrical processions through the city to present themselves in the best light, and also held parliament there during the 1450s. It seems that Lichfield Cathedral was included in this patronage early on, for in a transcription of an eye-witness record of furnishings and vestments compiled on 22 May 1445, just a month after the king and queen's marriage on 23 April, Henry and Margaret had already given red copes and altar dressings for the celebration of the coronation of the Virgin Mary held on 31 May: '2 copes of red tissue, on one the Salutation of St Mary on the upper shield, the other has the Coronation of St Mary on the shield, with cloth of that set for the altar above and below, given by King Henry VI and Margaret his consort.'[83]

OPPOSITE

The north window in St Mary's Guildhall, Coventry, dating to the mid-1450s and showing Henry VI in the centre, striking a pose worthy of Holbein. This is a key monument of the outbreak of the Wars of the Roses.

The full list helps us understand how the cathedral was presented. We can imagine worshippers entering the nave, beneath the screen of kings and saints on the west front, and seeing a central crucifix on the nave rood screen, the windows of the Lady Chapel beyond glowing with original glass. Some pilgrims would have climbed the steps, worn by the passage of two centuries, to the south transept doors, beneath a smaller gallery of sculpted figures. Inside, they looked up to see the head of God the Father presiding from the apex of the southern crossing arch and beyond it, the furthest boss of the north transept, a large red rose signifying Mary's blood sacrifice. A stone screen spanned the eastern crossing arch, flanked by the entrances to the aisles. Through here lay the riches described by the chronicler.

The choir was fitted with typical wooden seats and canopies, now lost without record, and we must imagine the air filled with resonant voices and light-rays shooting through the resinous smoke puffed from the swinging silver 'incense ship'. Approaching the climax of the Mass, all eyes looked east to the elevation of the host at the high altar, draped with a blue cloth like the Virgin's mantle and covered by a 150-year-old cloth of gold given by Walter Langton, presumably to accompany the magnificent altar cross.

In major processions, such as St Chad's day or Palm Sunday, when the cathedral came alive as the heavenly Jerusalem and the bishop was in attendance here rather than in Coventry, blue flashes would shoot from the two great sapphires set in the front and back of the bishop's mitre, together with garnets, topaz, amethyst and pearls, turquoise and emerald. Those close enough to study the silver gilt mount on his pastoral staff saw a depiction of a bishop genuflecting to St Mary. Behind the bishop and the dean, the canons wore white satin copes embroidered with stars and the letter 'M' for 'Mary' and crowned with gold, from a suite of 24 given before 1414.

In the feretory remained Langton's greatest gift:

1 large shrine of St Chad, between the high altar and the Chapel of St Mary, with large gilded images, and well decorated with various ornaments, having at the top upon the rood 1 large cockle with a man of silver gilt, brandishing a sword in his right hand, raised above him [this is St James 'the moor slayer', first apostle to be martyred, set between two other images of him; one being amongst the assumed twelve apostles in the Lady Chapel, the second, a martyr figure in the choir]. Item, on the front facing the altar 1 gold clasp, having in the middle 1 falcon enameled whitt, having in the circumference 8 clusters of large pearls, with a diamond in the middle of each cluster. Item, on the front facing the chapel there is a gold ring with a sapphire. Item, on the side of the shrine facing the chapel of St Nicholas [probably in the south choir aisle], 1 gold clasp well decorated with precious stones, fixed in the breast of an image of St Chad, and above the clasp 1 gold brooch, and 2 large crystals with 1 small block of crystal; and at the head of St Chad [1 gilded ring], and between the images on that side towards the chapel of St Nicholas are 7 rings or collars, partly gilded etc.[84]

A wall painting of the Holy Trinity, flanked by notably large angels, survives in the south choir aisle. The holes in the wall suggest there was once a canopied superstructure above it to shelter saintly relics, possibly St Chad's arm, positioned in relation both to the Head Chapel and the main shrine, and with the angels referencing Bede's account of Chad's death.

The shrine was railed in, presided over by a watching gallery reached by a staircase in the north-west corner of the Lady Chapel. Scars on the masonry of the southern main arcade piers show that a tomb was set up here, which may have been Langton's, or more probably Northburgh's, if Langton chose the recess off his Lady Chapel.

In the sacrist's house was an elaborate portable gilded and pearl-studded shrine combining the evangelists Mark and Luke with a crucifix and branches of coral, and a sapphire 'over an inch long'. This was likely to be St Chad's head shrine. His arm was displayed in a silver-gilt sheath standing on three lions, perhaps in the south choir aisle, where a late medieval wall painting of the Trinity (which may date to c.1450) remains beneath disused mural sockets for a canopied superstructure.[85] An arm of St Sampson was similarly encased in silver gilt.

OPPOSITE
Long before the Victorian alabaster reredos, an early-fifteenth century screen stood here to frame the golden altar furniture, including the relic of the cross. Only a few fragments of it remain.

OPPOSITE

The two courtyards
of the Vicars' Choral
(now Vicars' Close)
were reached via the
west gate, which had
been completed by
the middle of the
fourteenth century
and by 1530 carried
a statue of the Virgin
Mary. The timber-
framed houses were
constructed between
c.1315 and c.1500, when
this row was built.

RIGHT

Vicars' Close features
a fine array of
domestic buildings
spanning several
styles and centuries,
mostly in brick and
timber. Newton's
College (left) was
built in stone from
1800–1806 as the gift
of John Newton. It
replaced the remains
of the medieval west
gate, to better frame
views of the cathedral.

We may recently have encountered members of the audience for this liturgical drama. In summer 2015 numerous skeletons were found in the grounds of St John's Hospital, which once hosted visitors seeking cures from affliction and a guarantee of salvation. They may have responded to a decree of 1476, that indulgences were transferable to the afterlife of the dead in purgatory, spurring pilgrimages on behalf of deceased family members. Shortly after, in 1483, the chapter decreed that profits from the offerings at the statues of Christ and St Anne (Mary's mother), made in the fine lost confraternity chantry that Dean Heywood established in 1468, should be given to the embellishment of the altar and thereafter to the fabric fund.[86] What was being planned? By 1490 a new library was under way to the north of the nave. It was completed by 1500 under Dean Yotton, whose memorial remains facing his achievement, the spandrels filled with grapevines.

The timber-framed lodgings in the Vicars' Close were rebuilt by this time, as the incumbents demanded more independence and better working conditions. And luck was on their side for a while. Lichfield had a 300-year-long special relationship with the English monarchy and now a benevolent royal administrator arrived, in the figure of James Denton, dean 1522–33. Denton was chancellor to Mary Tudor, sister of Henry VIII and queen of France, and chaplain to Henry VIII. At St George's Chapel, Windsor, he built 'Denton's Commons' as accommodation for choristers and chantry priests, and he provided similar buildings at Lichfield, heralded by a gate to the close decorated with his arms, through which visitors passed until its demolition in 1776. For anyone who followed the road into Lichfield city on a wet day, the roof over the market cross offered shelter 'for poor folks to stand dry in'. Denton paid £160 to provide it.

James Denton's 'Black Book' survives at Windsor, beautifully illuminated. On its cover page is a red rose symbolizing the king – but this is as nothing compared to the carved Marian rose beneath Lichfield's south-west tower, plugging the bell-rope oculus in Denton's vault (see p. 51). The vault bosses show his rebus, a pictogram with a scallop shell (St James), and a leafy den in which lies a 'tun'. Amongst the surrounding bosses are a dragon, a bearded unicorn (robbed of its horn) and grape vines. The story they tell was even then an ancient one: the fight between biblical good and evil. The unicorn, also portrayed on tapestries of the time, is a symbol of Christ and from its blood came salvation. This message reconciled the cathedral's prevalent themes and imagery, but within a decade an act of salvation was needed to spare the building itself.

OPPOSITE
The nave is a
miraculous survival.
The Civil War
bombardment and
roof stripping failed
to collapse its bowing
vaults, which were
replaced from 1789.
The aisle arcades have
been heavily restored,
but much other
sculpture was simply
out of reach.

BELOW RIGHT
St Mary's cathedral
priory, Coventry;
the remains of the
interior of the west
front. The church and
monastic buildings
were destroyed in
favour of retaining
Lichfield as sole
cathedral for the
diocese. The site
became a graveyard.

PREVIOUS SPREAD
The eastern limb
of the cathedral
contained immense
riches, but its shrines
and altar dressings
were grasped by
Henry VIII during
the Reformation and
tombs were smashed
and looted by Civil
War troops a century
later. The denuded
cathedral was re-
dressed in the later
nineteenth century
with rich carving and
encaustic tiles.

4

Dissolution, Civil War and the Road to Recovery

The reign of Henry VIII is usually divided into two halves, pivoting at the break with papal Rome in 1534. In the king's early years, as an ardent inheritor of the Marian cult, his anti-Lutheran rhetoric won him the title 'Defender of the Faith' from Pope Leo X; after the break, the antagonism with all Europe's great powers led his commissioners to empty the riches of the great churches into the royal coffers, so that fortresses and warships might better defend the English Channel. English cathedrals, many of which were monastic foundations, generally fared worse during the dissolution of the monasteries than in the Civil War a century later. Lichfield was the outstanding exception.

The only cathedral to be wholly destroyed as part of Henry VIII's reforms was in the diocese of Coventry and Lichfield; in 1541 the decision was made to dissolve St Mary's Coventry, perhaps because of its monastic community, or reflecting Lichfield's pro-royal record. But Lichfield did not escape sanctioned pillage. The king's men, journeying with

tools and carts, had arrived in 1538 to break up Chad's shrines. Unusually, while the commissioners took statues, jewels and metals, Henry VIII granted Bishop Lee permission to adapt St Chad's shrine for its own purposes, from which we might assume that the base remained. Some of the bones of St Chad were removed and smuggled out by Canon Arthur Dudley, to begin their own journey to Birmingham Cathedral. In March 1548, a year into the reign of Edward VI and his Protestant

protectors, 17 chantries, serviced at 13 altars, were dissolved; Lichfield's martyrial imagery was now transferred to the city's arms.

There is no evidence to suggest that the cathedral's architecture was otherwise affected. Ahead lay a century of respite – even though religious strife divided Protestants from Catholic recusants to create new martyrs in the Market Square – before serious trouble was fomented between the Stuart kings and parliament. Quietly the cathedral presided over a market city, within the safety of its old, defensible walls.

Antiquarianism was on the rise by the Elizabethan era; no doubt the nostalgic lament for 'bare ruined choirs' led to urgency to record and salvage what might otherwise be lost. The historian William Camden (1551–1623) was born to parents from Lichfield; Sampson Camden was a paper-stainer, who went to London two centuries before Samuel Johnson took the same road. In 1600 Sampson Erdeswicke, the antiquarian and surveyor of Staffordshire, wrote in admiration of Lichfield's steeples, 'curiously wrought'. He thought the west front:

> exceedingly finely and cunningly set forth, with a great number of Tabernacles, and in the same, the images, or pictures of the Prophets, Apostles, Kings of Judah and diverse other kings of this Land, so well embossed, and so lively cut, that it is a great pleasure for any Man that takes delight in rarities, to behold them.[88]

Inside, past 'fair pillars and rich windows' the vestry still held 'old, rich copes' and an improbably ostentatious communion cloth, made of cloth of gold. Perhaps Langton's corporal (altar cloth) had found new life within the building Daniel King depicted in engravings just before devastation came to town.

ABOVE
The city's arms bearing the severed limbs of martyrdom.

OPPOSITE
The cathedral from the south-west, showing the higher medieval roof-lines, framed by the inverted 'V' mouldings of the tower conforming to the height of the gables. These were lost to missiles and lead-stripping profiteers.

The Civil War Arrives

THE CIVIL WAR IN LICHFIELD BROUGHT THE UTTER RUINATION OF THE cathedral: or rather, that is the popular perception. The sieges of the 1640s certainly affected it more than any other cathedral; bombardment smashed the glass and damaged the roofs and central spire so heavily that two decades of rain fell on the vaults, dampening both the stonework and the public impression of a great building. But the belief that its medieval architecture was mostly destroyed by iconoclasts and cannonballs is inaccurate. Much of the building survived the onslaught, and the damage inspired an unusual level of care in the restoration of its fabric.

As Charles I moved north from London in 1642, the battle lines of the Civil War were drawn across the Midlands, where Edgehill was the first engagement on Sunday 23 October, just 45 miles south of Lichfield. Having taken Stratford-upon-Avon that winter, the parliamentarian forces arrived on 2 March 1643, led by Robert Grevill, 2nd Baron Brooke, an ardent puritan who had published his criticism of bishops. A royalist

RIGHT
Shown as a vision of
bucolic peace at the
restoration of the
cathedral's fabric,
the city's distinctive
spires preside over
the landscape for
miles around in this
late-seventeenth-
century print.

sniper watched them approach along Dam Street; he was 'posted in the leads',[89] probably crouching behind the stone parapets of the cathedral tower. This was the highest vantage point in the fortified close, garrisoned by the earl of Chesterfield and Sir Richard Dyott. The sniper aimed his gun barrel, squeezed the trigger and Lord Brooke fell dead from a wound through the forehead. Before the end of the century Anthony Wood (1632–95) attributed the shot to 'Diot', presumably John Dyott, Sir Richard's son, deaf and dumb but given eagle eyes or cat's lives.[90]

It did not escape notice that this was St Chad's day, which savoured of deliverance. Any triumphalism was short-lived, however, for the parliamentarians took the cathedral almost immediately, stabled their horses in it, and, as Dugdale tells us:

> Broke up the pavement, polluted the choir with their excrements, every day hunted a cat with hounds throughout the church, delighting themselves in the echo from the goodly vaulted roof, and to add to their wickedness brought a calf into it wrapped in linen, carried it to the font sprinkled it with water, and gave it a name in scorn and derision of the that holy sacrament of baptism.

The final bombardment from March to July 1646 was the most severe. 'Two thousand shots of great ordnance and one thousand five hundred grenadoes' ripped through the roof timbers and brought the cap of the great spire crashing down on the Head Chapel, and perhaps partly on the north transept. The south-west spire was also severely damaged and the impression from afar must have been grievous. Whatever remained of the medieval window glass was hopelessly vulnerable. Yet the thick vaults substantially withstood the onslaught, protecting the carved stonework. The survival of the tympana of Christ on the west front and in the chapter house, along with numerous sculptures, confirm that the internal destruction was due less to religious feeling than to profiteering. The library was ransacked; 67 gravestones lost their brasswork; 100 coats of arms were destroyed, as were five chest tombs of bishops. The wreckers' discovery of Bishop Scrope's chalice and crosier confirmed that treasure lay beneath the flagstones and tiles. Riches also lay above in the form of lead sheet, the remains of which were stripped from the roofs to fetch £1,200 in 1651. The vaults were now open to soaking rain and frost.

The Bishop's Palace with Langton's magnificent murals lay ruined, the defences and turrets blown up or torn down. Not since Coventry's dissolution a century earlier had anyone seen a cathedral so 'exceedingly ruinated'. Services were held in the chapter house for shelter, while the great building became a quarry; in 1651 its carcass was pulled apart to keep the poor in work.

Catholic recusants understood what survived of Lichfield's imagery and held it in high esteem. By this time the wounded Christ in the western gable had been spirited off to Swynnerton by the Fitzherbert family (see p. 75). On the other side of the religious divide, George Fox (1624–91), founder of the Quakers, came to Lichfield in 1651. His account explicitly relates the cathedral's tradition of Roman martyrdom to the more recent blood sacrifice:

> AND as I was walking along with several friends, I lifted up my head, and I saw three steeple-house spires, and they struck at my life; and I asked friends what place that was, and they said Lichfield; immediately the word of the Lord came to me, that I must go thither [...] as soon as I was got within the city, the word of the Lord came to me again, saying, "Cry, Woe unto the bloody city of Lichfield." So I went up and down the streets, crying with a loud voice, "Woe to the bloody city of Lichfield!" [...] Ancient records testify how many of the Christian Britons suffered there; and much I could write of the sense I had of the blood of the martyrs that hath been shed in this nation, for the name of Christ. [91]

The cathedral's spires were actually broken at the time he visited, and must have resembled martyrs themselves. But although its old identity was ebbing away in the common memory, this admired great building was not beyond rescue.

The Road to Recovery after 1660

A FORLORN LICHFIELD CATHEDRAL HAD KNOWN A HISTORY OF ALMOST A thousand years when Charles II restored the monarchy in 1660. The two centuries following his coronation chart the cathedral's own restoration. There were many disputes about the treatment it should receive but letters between the chapter and architects, as well as diarists' accounts, reveal a shared respect for its distinctive shape, consummate craftsmanship and the traditions it represented. Its unbroken use continued through the Age of Reason, when Samuel Johnson's wit and learning illuminated the city. As an intellectual centre and marketplace on the coaching roads to Liverpool, Lichfield was largely bypassed by the era of industry and the advent of mainline railways, which better preserves the city and the cathedral's setting today.

'One of the finest and most beautiful in England, especially for the outside, the form and figure of the building, the carv'd work'd, imagery, and the three beautiful spires; the like of which are not to be seen in one church, no, not in Europe.' So said Daniel Defoe of Lichfield Cathedral, as he arrived on horseback around 1720 to admire its ancient form, though not all that the writer saw was the work of ancient hands. He was viewing a restoration reputed to have cost £20,000, with as many man-hours of effort expended on this vision of serenity. The credit for the recovery from the barrage of the 1640s was shared. Elias Ashmole sequestered numerous books from Lichfield's raided library, while Precentor William Higgins, who rescued the Lichfield Gospels, took practical repairs into his own hands.

From the restoration of the monarchy under Charles II in 1660, official reparation efforts concerned not only the improvement of the torn building, but also the rehabilitation of the old order it represented. The antiquarian William Dugdale canvassed this from the outset, and the momentum was picked up by Dean William Paul from February 1661 and by Bishop Hacket who, when he finally arrived in August 'on the very next day after his arrival, he set his coach-horses, with teams, to remove the rubbish'. His fundraising schemes included sponsorship of the choirstalls at £8 apiece.[92]

Major repairs required substantial scaffolding for roof assembly, masonry repairs and an acre or so of glazing. Five bosses in the north transept suggest some rebuilding of the vaulting, as their crudeness matches stonework surrounding the west window, being curious interpretations of medieval leaf carving. The arches of the four western bays of the choir were also blocked up. Whether due to efficiency, intensive labour or the speed afforded by ersatz imitation, this repair was rapid. The transepts were glazed during 1663, and the entire main body of the cathedral roofed and leaded two years later. In 1666, the central spire and west window tracery were both in place, the latter looking more like the currently admired west window of Exeter Cathedral than an archaeological replacement of Lichfield's original model. Hacket told Shelton that 'we have at Lichfield the stateliest spire and goodliest window in stone to the west that is in England' adding 'I would they were paid for'. Their triumph was surmounted by a standing figure beneath a canopy by Sir William Wilson, thought by Pennant to be 'a very bad one of *Charles* II who had contributed to the repair of the church, by a liberal gift of timber'.

The king had indeed given a hundred oaks, a major contribution to what remains the best suite of seventeenth-century cathedral roofs in Britain beyond St Paul's. The work may have included the unique wheel of stone balusters replacing the tracery of the medieval rose window in the south transept. That figure of Charles II survives, weathered and demoted to the south-west angle of the south transept. Its original, oddly chunky stone canopy was rediscovered in 1932 and mistakenly proclaimed to be a Saxon throne.

LEFT
Charles II, removed from the late seventeenth-century west front gable where he had assumed the position originally taken by Christ, and now relegated to the south transept.

OPPOSITE
With the restoration of the monarchy in 1660, services were again resumed.

LEFT
The Bishop's Palace
was built for Thomas
Wood as a modern
replacement for the
ruined medieval
palace; the wings are a
later but sympathetic
addition.

OPPOSITE
The bowing of the
nave parapets and
the lower pitch of the
seventeenth-century
trusses are clearly
visible in this roof
view.

By contrast, Langton's shattered old palace was well beyond recovery. Bishop Thomas Wood (1671–92) saw to replacing it with a new bishop's residence to a design by Edward Pierce, a follower of Christopher Wren. The pedimented façade is a confident monument of its own era, without military triumphalism, yet it proved unpopular and was let to tenants, its residents including the writer Anna Seward, whose father was a canon residentiary. She remained here until her death in 1809, looking onto the complex massing of the north side through 20,000 days, and wrote:

> High o'er proud towns where Gothic structures rise,
> How rare the freshness of unsullied skies!
> Oft cling to choral walls the mansions vile,
> Unseemly blots upon the graceful pile!
> Here not one squalid, mouldering cell appears,
> To mar the splendid toil of ancient years
>
> Anna Seward, from *Lichfield, An Elegy*, May 1781

In contrast to the houses once clustered against St Michael's, Coventry, for example, this 'pile' was unmarred, owing to a lack of industry, the suburban isolation provided by 16 acres of close and a general admiration for the sublime in the era of the 'Picturesque'. Horace Walpole's observation of 1760 that 'nothing is left in the inside of ornament' was patently untrue, though understandable if he were comparing its depredations to most other cathedrals. Certainly a further refurbishment was pending. Lichfield's later eighteenth-

ABOVE
The close has the
atmosphere of a
country town.

OPPOSITE
James Wyatt inserted
a screen in the
eastern crossing
arch, of which
no trace remains,
and Lichfield now
represents the best-
surviving cathedral
refurbishment by
George Gilbert Scott.
To the few years
before 1861 we owe
the (resituated) organ,
restored statuary,
choir furnishings and
screen. Later came
the west window
(c.1868–69) and the
gradual insertion of
stained glass. Less
obvious was Scott's
removal of poor
cement restorations
by Robert Armstrong.

century restorers were concerned with the maintenance of its surviving medieval fabric, while seeking to make the practical improvements demanded by the chapter. Often the latter won out, seeking comforts foreign to the building's formative Catholic culture as a pilgrimage centre. Thomas Pennant used Lichfield to explain this paradoxical empathy in the Age of Reason: 'All the fine arts of past times, and all the magnificent works we now so justly admire, are owing to a species of piety that every lover of the elegance of architecture must rejoice to have existed.'

The architect James Wyatt (1746–1813), who was of Staffordshire origin, was extracted with reluctance from his London office to refurbish the cathedral, following local masons' competent restorations of the walls. From 1787 to 1792 he worked on a cathedral 'not greatly out of repair'. The clergy had lately joined the parishioners in the crammed nave because the choir was inhospitable and cold. Wyatt therefore considered it necessary to dismantle the late medieval reredos and extend the choir over the site of St Chad's shrine and through the Lady Chapel, to focus on a new altar and east window there, making it 'one of the most beautiful choirs in the kingdom'. Unhappily the distance to the Lady Chapel altar created the 'singular and unexpected effect of preventing the preacher being heard'. Wyatt contained this refurbishment within curtained windows to reduce light and improve insulation, helped by a tall glazed screen at the crossing. This inauthentic spatial division was later deplored by Pugin, among others, but for now the chapter held the cathedral to be 'greatly beautified and ornamented'.

The clearance of the nave enabled its closer inspection. Most obviously, its glassy clerestory had been pushed outward over 0.3 m (1 ft) on each side by the nave's stone high vaults, estimated to weigh 500 tons. As Hereford Cathedral's west front had recently collapsed, Wyatt recommended taking no chances, so workmen dismantled and replaced nave bays 2 to 6, leaving the ends (1 and 7) to brace the west front and central tower. His replacements were sturdy oak ribs, the ridge-ribs decorated with uniform stiff-leaf carving, and plaster webs offering 'not now one twentieth part of the weight to sustain'. The accounts for this work span 4 November 1788 to 1 September 1790, and also detail the reinstating of the medieval pitch of the aisle roofs to prop the clerestory walls efficiently. By 1792 £7,000 had been spent on work, including the replacement of the buttresses of the south transept and the dismantling and rebuilding of the central spire, barely a century old. Wyatt must be acknowledged as saving the nave, and possibly also the spire, from collapse but, less commendably, he gave away the last known stone fragment from Chad's

RIGHT

A thirteenth-century figure of St Peter is entombed within this cladding of Roman cement, a well-intended restoration more probably by Robert Armstrong than by Wyatt's collaborator, Bernasconi.

shrine to ornament an acquaintance's stable, and it has now been lost.

Wyatt's deputy was Joseph Potter senior, who was paid a 'bounty' of £50 for his fastidiousness in Wyatt's conspicuous absence. Potter went on to supervise work to the north transept vault and roofs in 1793 before tackling the west front in 1820, where he attempted to keep the weathered medieval statuary, coating and remodelling them with Roman cement which solidified into unmistakably post-medieval facial expressions. Examples of such figures from c.1240, probably from the south transept, remain in the central tower and the chapter house vestibule.

The most spectacular addition to the cathedral under Potter's tenure was the installation of sixteenth-century glass, brought 400 miles from Herkenrode Abbey (now Belgium) and installed after 1804 (see Appendix). Perhaps ironically, Wyatt's inauthentic choir arrangement framed this repatriation of late medieval imagery and colour with a drama that justified the expense.

Between 1800 and 1842, the fabric account bill totalled £41,000. By then, Victorian taste decried Wyatt's interventions and Georgian dramas; a more archaeological approach to medieval buildings often imbued decisions with scholarship, and sometimes with preciousness. Sydney Smirke took Potter's place in 1842 as an architect 'of sound judgement and experience in ecclesiastical architecture'. Two years later he structurally reinforced the south side of the nave, where 'I have continued to restore scrupulously to the best of my belief the original forms of the building, but in the clerestory parapet and in the buttress heads I have been compelled to exercise some freedom'. In 1854 he mentioned that the sculpted details in the nave were being cleaned of plaster and whitewash 'bringing out the beautiful [thirteenth-century] carving that ornaments this arcade'. He went on to the north transept, refacing all the masonry in Tixall stone 'exactly as before in all those parts that are of medieval date' without touching the rich north portal. Smirke also took down Wyatt's choir enclosures, but he resigned over disputes about direction when George Gilbert Scott senior arrived on the scene in 1857.

ANNO   1332

ABOVE & LEFT

The sixteenth-century stained glass at Lichfield came from Herkenrode Abbey in Flanders but its themes would have been recognizable to contemporaries in Lichfield during the age of Henry VIII (1509–47), especially to those who knew King's College Chapel in Cambridge. These details show the Virgin and Child (top); St John the Evangelist (left), purported author of the Book of Revelation, and the Last Judgment (far left) from the same book, showing Christ separating the saved from the damned (see Appendix).

ABOVE

Kempe's late
Victorian reredos
of Tutbury alabaster.
Its popularity was
short-lived, but it
has nonetheless
enjoyed longevity.

Smirke had sought to restore what he found of the medieval work, irrespective of style, because cathedrals had, after all, evolved. By contrast Scott was a purist at heart, wanting 'to restore the building to the state in which it had existed in better times of ecclesiastical architecture', by reversing Wyatt and Potter's work and also some of Smirke's repairs. There were limitations to his ambition, however; Wyatt's judiciously light nave vault remains; and as time can never truly be reversed, so Scott inevitably imposed his own sensibility and choice of materials. He heavily restored the nave aisle arcades in c.1868–72, his sculpted hoodmould bosses brandishing a typical Prince Albert-as-Ivanhoe physiognomy. Whereas Smirke had argued that the reredos of c.1400, removed by Wyatt, should be replaced in original style, Scott followed the accepted idea that thirteenth-century architecture was superior, irrespective of evidence. The result, conceived by Scott as a paraphrase of Westminster Abbey's thirteenth-century retable but apparently redesigned and executed under C.E. Kempe in the 1890s, cannot be confused with medieval work. It is composed of Tutbury alabaster and materials from the diocese, costing £2,000.

The new choir furniture, devoid of the canopies typical of choirstalls, was made by 'Mr Evans of Ellastone'. Scott unblocked the filled-in south transept windows and replaced the seventeenth-century great west window with one of his several variant designs, while his painted iron pulpitum screen, co-designed by J.B. Phillips and made by Skidmore of Coventry, was deemed 'the first screen of this kind'[93] in the Victorian era, intended to 'render every part available for worship'.[94] The pulpit is studded with stone bosses, explained as 'undoubtedly unique of its kind'[95] and compared with the medieval silver pulpit of Aix-la-Chapelle and metalwork in Venice and Nuremberg. It was certainly a fine piece, typical of its age, of a type that rapidly became unfashionable but has since recovered its admirers.

OPPOSITE & BELOW
LEFT

Scott's use of painted
iron for the pulpitum
screen drew on
the precedent of
medieval grilles,
while the choice of
tracery and roses
betrays an informed
sensibility for this
early fourteenth-
century limb of a
Marian church and
the angelic choir
complements the
sound of song and
organ pipes.

BELOW RIGHT

The pulpit is notably
exotic, its precious
metals and studded
stones evoking
the lost riches of
medieval Lichfield.
A brass relief shows
St Peter preaching
at Pentecost, while
the eagle lectern is
by the Birmingham
company of John
Hardman & Co.

The marvel is that Lichfield retains an unusually intact Scott scheme, as his other mid-Victorian cathedral refurbishments were dismantled. The result is a cathedral whose interior reads from end to end without the interruptions of its medieval nave altar, pulpitum, choir stalls and reredos, being unified by Scott's floors of Hopton wood and blue lias stones, a strictly inauthentic but certainly impressive vista that admits the reality of its historical revisions. Henry James wrote that 'there is something grandly elegant in the unity of effect produced by this unobstructed perspective'.[96]

At precisely the time of Scott's campaign, cathedral guides began to be written for popular reference and Lichfield was celebrated as one of the most perfect works of architecture in the Midlands, an object of considerable interest to residents in the locality as well as to visitors now arriving by rail. From J.B. Stone's history in 1870, we are offered not just attempts at the archaeological assessment of the building's evolution, with the observations of Robert Willis, but a contemporary assessment of restorers' works in progress. This is a happy circumstance that not only documented observations on the Victorian work, but recorded shifting attitudes.

Scott's son, John Oldrid Scott, began to restore the ragged west front in 1878, transforming what seemed to Henry James to be 'covered in stucco and paint', a magnificent accomplishment of Victorian sculpture best explained by labelling the statuary. His further work in the north transept revealed that the heads of five thirteenth-century lancet window arches survived above a later broader window, which provided the rare opportunity for a demonstrably accurate restoration. This example was not followed in the south transept, where the fifteenth-century window pattern offered a screen for luminous stained glass by Kempe. By the time this was installed, c.1890, the cathedral had essentially become the grand, fragmentary, tantalizing vision that we recognize today. The twentieth century largely bypassed Lichfield on its branch railway line, and as wars came and went, the cathedral was carefully repaired and services were maintained in its green, domesticated close, avoiding much attention.

In 1974, Pevsner's *Buildings of England* volume on Staffordshire explained that 'much of the cathedral as we see it today is Scott's, not only mouldings, capitals, and statues, but also most of the window tracery. The question how far it replaced accurately what had been there in the Middle Ages has never been adequately answered, and so no answer can be attempted here'.[97]

A decade or so later, research showed that Scott's hand had been constrained to 'preserve the greatest possible amount of old work', so that in the south transept he 'had to put everything back "as before" but in new stone'.[98] Typically, at least one original stone was retained, as respectful witness for each restored feature.

Lichfield Cathedral remains wholly underestimated, and hence this book has attempted to better understand it. There is much still to learn of this great building, which will undoubtedly continue to surprise and intrigue all who come to explore it, glimpsing what they can of its immense past and the meanings it held for our ancestors.

OPPOSITE
The nave is not accurately aligned with the east end; no doubt this mattered less when a rood and stone pulpitum screen and banners broke the perspective.

OVERLEAF
The west front has been subject to intense damage and restoration, so that only five early-fourteenth-century figures remain, on the north-west tower. Some others were removed in 1749 and Robert Armstrong undertook the surface remodelling of the remainder with cement, achieving crude simulacra; much of this was done c.1820–22. Victorian restorers disputed the attributions for many of the original characters and themes, rejecting the idea of Jewish kings in favour of St Chad in the centre, flanked by Anglo-Saxon kings suited to this ancient kingdom, and post-Norman conquest kings in the manner of other (later) cathedral façades.

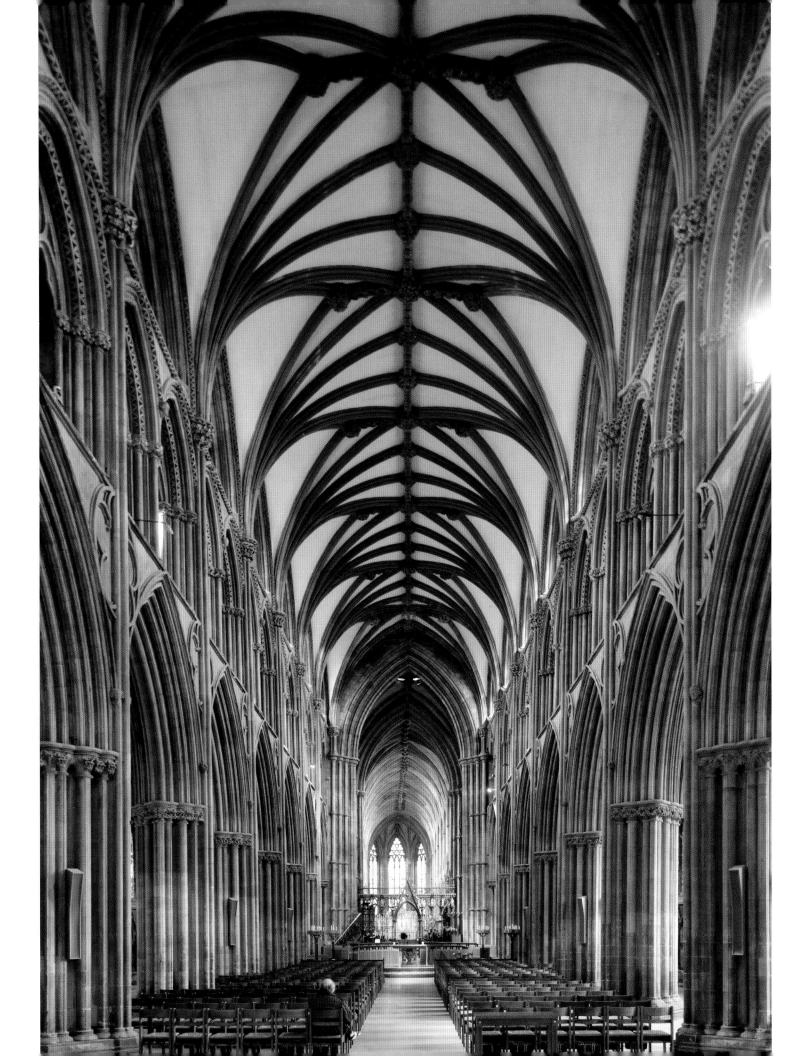

The present tally of 113 west front figures is given below, reading from top left, with symbolic attributes. Most are restorations of c.1876–84, supervised by George Gilbert Scott (d. 1878) and his son John Oldrid Scott, who was solely responsible from 1878 to 1901. They were carved by Robert Bridgeman & Son; finer portal figures are by Mary Grant, while Queen Victoria is by Princess Louise, Duchess of Argyle (1848–1939).

1 NORTH-WEST TOWER, UPPER STAGE, FEMALE FIGURES AND PROPHETS
Eve (spinning distaff); unattributed medieval figure; Sarah (cakes); Rebekah (jar); Rachel (shepherd's crook); Deborah (scroll); unattributed medieval figure; Hannah (Samuel as a child); Samuel (scroll); Aaron (scroll); unattributed medieval figure; unattributed medieval figure

2 GABLE, CHRIST AND ARCHANGELS
Christ blessing; Moses (tablets), Elijah (book); Gabriel (lily); Uriel (open book); Michael (lance and serpent); Raphael (pilgrim's staff)

3 SOUTH-WEST TOWER, UPPER STAGE, OLD TESTAMENT PATRIARCHS
Adam (lion); Abel (lamb and crook); Abraham (fire and knife); Isaac (prayer); Jacob (staff); Melchizedek (censer); Enoch (scroll); Methuselah (staff); Noah (ark and olive branch); Daniel (pen and scroll); Job (staff); Shem (drapery)

4 NORTH-WEST TOWER TURRET, MIDDLE STAGE, MISCELLANEOUS
St Edith/Eadgyth of Wilton (crown, staff and book); David (crown and harp); St Helena (tower and cross); Solomon (sceptre and temple); Edward Bickersteth, Dean of Lichfield (cathedral); St Mark (lion, book); Queen Victoria (orb and sceptre); St Luke (staff, serpent)

5 NORTH SIDE OF MAIN FRONT, MIDDLE STAGE, PROPHETS AND ARCHANGELS
Gabriel (shield, sceptre); Zechariah (candle, scroll); Nahum (scroll); Amos (crook and branch); Jeremiah (stands on ruined temple); Uriel (spear); Malachi (fire and scroll); Habakkuk (tablet and tower); Obadiah (scroll); Daniel (scroll and fire)

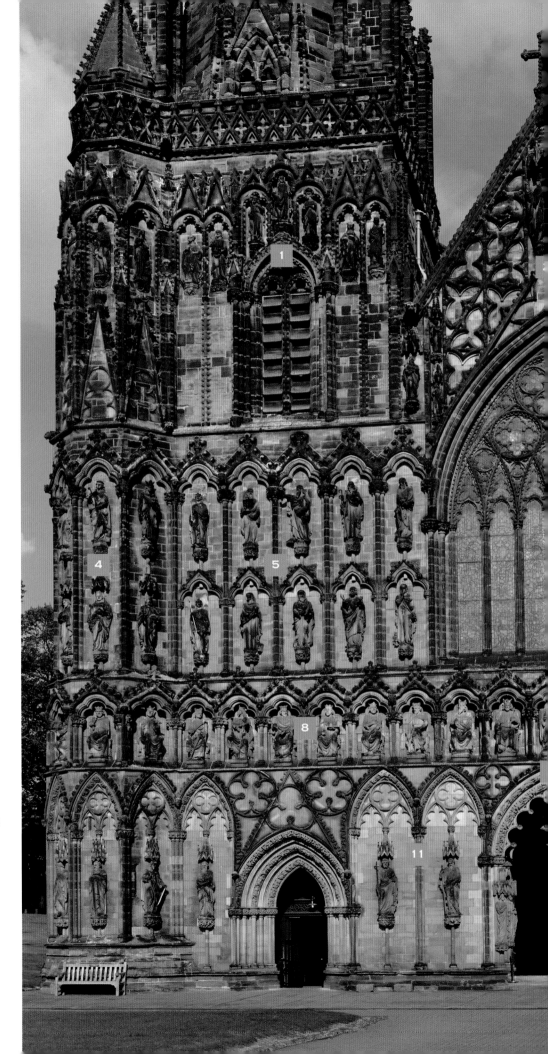

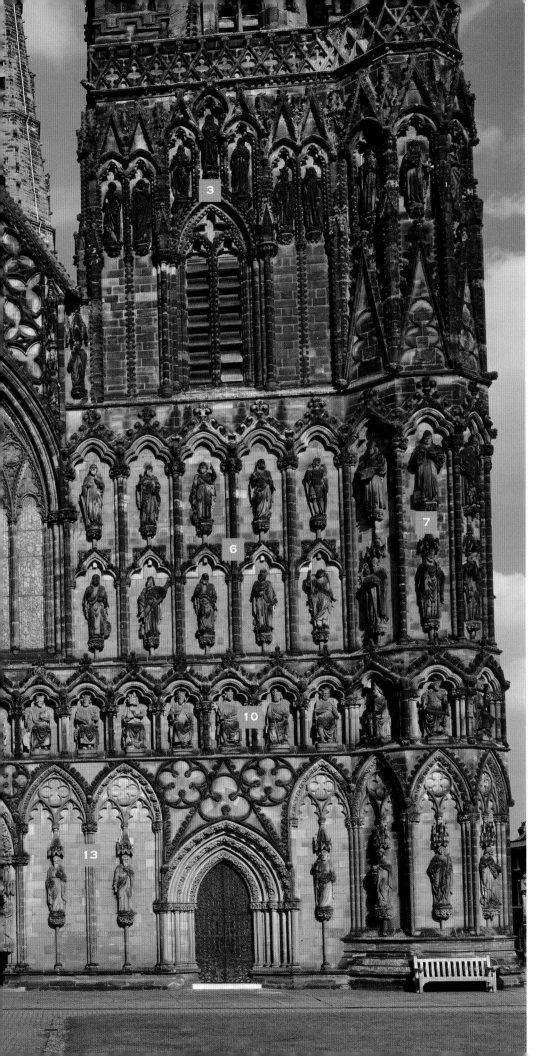

6 SOUTH SIDE, MIDDLE STAGE, PROPHETS AND ARCHANGELS

Isaiah (saw); Zephaniah (torch); Jonah (fish); Hosea (skull); St Michael (armoured); Ezekiel (wheel); Haggai (part of the temple); Micah (treading on idol); Joel (locusts); St Raphael (pilgrim staff)

7 SOUTH-WEST TOWER TURRET, MIDDLE STAGE, BISHOPS, MOSTLY OF LICHFIELD

John Hacket (1661–70); John Lonsdale (1843–67); George A. Selwyn (1868–78); William Maclagan, Archbishop of York (1891–1908); Roger de Clinton (1129–48); Patteshull (1240–41); Walter Langton (1296–1321); Theodore of Tarsus, Archbishop of Canterbury (668–690)

8 NORTH SIDE, LOWER STAGE, KINGS AFTER 1066

William I; William II; Henry I; Stephen of Blois; Henry II; Richard I; John; Henry III; Edward I; Edward II; Edward III; Richard II

9 CENTRE, LOWER STAGE

Chad, bishop of Lichfield (669–72)

10 SOUTH SIDE, LOWER STAGE, ANGLO-SAXON KINGS

Peada; Wulfhere; Ethelred; Offa; Egbert; Ethelwolf; Ethelbert; Ethelred; Alfred 'the Great'; Edgar; Canute; Edward the Confessor

11 NORTH SIDE, GROUND STAGE, APOSTLES AND SAINTS

St Cyprian (bishop's mitre, sword and book); St Bartholomew (knife); St Simon the Zealot (saw); St James the Less (club and book); St Thomas (set square); St Philip (cross and book; St Andrew (X-cross); St John the Evangelist (pen and book); St. Matthias (book and staff)

12 BENEATH CHAD, WITHIN THE CENTRAL PORTAL

Christ in the tympanum, c.1290–1300; from left, Mary Magdalene (ointment); Virgin and Child; Mary of Clopas

13 SOUTH SIDE, GROUND STAGE, APOSTLES AND SAINTS

St Barnabas (stone); St Peter (keys and book); St Paul (sword and book); St Matthew (wallet); St James the Greater (staff, book and shell); St Jude (scroll); St Stephen (stones and palm leaf); St Clement (anchor and book); St Werburga (staff, book and demoted crown)

113

Appendix
The Herkenrode Glass

THE CIVIL WAR SAW THE CATHEDRAL ransacked, its stained glass smashed and then replaced by plain quarries. Glazed imagery returned in the later eighteenth century, when Francis Eginton designed a new east window for James Wyatt's remodelled Lady Chapel on the theme of the resurrection, after a design by Joshua Reynolds. That was short-lived for, in June 1803, Lichfield Cathedral received a consignment of 340 panels of extremely fine, salvaged, mid-sixteenth-century stained glass shipped from the continent. Their reuse here represents the greatest display of imported, ex-situ stained glass in Britain.

Lichfield's Renaissance-era stained glass, with its vivid colours, fine heraldry and classical architecture, came from Herkenrode Abbey, a monastery of Cistercian nuns in the province of Limburg, in modern Belgium. The panels date to between 1532 and 1539 and were originally made by the workshop of master glaziers Martin Tymus (or 'Tymans' or 'Temes') of Antwerp and possibly Lambert Spulberch of Malines. Of the 12 windows that feature Herkenrode glass, the seven most substantial are in the Lady Chapel. Two more panels are in the choir ambulatory, some glass features in both north and south choir aisles and there is another example in the south-east window of the south transept.

Medieval Herkenrode Abbey and its accumulation of artistic treasures was liquidated after the French Revolution; the new republic rejected religious communities and their estates were placed under 'protection'. The monastery was dissolved by a decree of 1 January 1793, which was enforced on 12 December 1796, when the nuns left. The purchasers of the abbey church, Pierre Libotton and Guillaume Claes of Hasselt, stripped the building for use as a textile factory, which in turn was gutted by a fire in 1826, and then demolished in 1843. Excavations in 1973 showed the church featured a five-sided apse, a coincidental similarity to Lichfield's polygonal eastern termination.

The majority of Herkenrode's coloured glass, a parcel of 340 panels, was sold to Sir Brooke Boothby of Ashbourne (1744-1821), who offered it on resale to Lichfield Cathedral for £200, in reimbursement of the purchase price. The chapter paid Boothby in instalments between 1801 and 1804, and the parcels were opened here in June 1803. They would discover the total cost to be £800 with shipping, repair and installation.

It is easy to forget the logistical triumph of shipping ancient glass over sea and land without its shattering (though some was indeed found to have broken on arrival). Skillful, too, was the arrangement designed by Rev. W.G. Rowland of St Mary's, Shrewsbury, which enabled the panels to fit into Lichfield's Lady Chapel so remarkably well, with the necessary adjustments being made by the firm of Betton and Evans (who may be responsible for inserting some spare Herkenrode glass in Rowland's own church). More obviously, these windows display a richness and quality of which the chapel's original munificent founder, Bishop Langton, is likely to have approved.

The glass in the Lady Chapel was cleaned and restored by Bridgeman's between 1887 and 1892, and taken down for storage in the Anglesey vault in September 1939, to be reinstated after the end of the Second World War in October 1945. The windows were more recently conserved and repaired by Barley Studio between 2010 and 2015.

The Herkenrode glass is difficult to understand, partly because of its intrinsic complexity and myriad details, and also because it does not represent an original arrangement. Late medieval glass usually portrayed the narrative of creation on the north side, the expulsion from Paradise being answered by salvation through crucifixion in the focal east window. Here, a mystery endures. When the parcels were opened at Lichfield, the fifteen-panel scene of the crucifixion was missing. Other than some possibly related fragments in the south quire aisle, they have never been traced.

The key on the following pages aims to make its imagery as comprehensible as possible.

WINDOW NORTH IV
FOUR DONORS

1

In this excellent
window, the arms
of Jean de Hornes,
provost of Liège,
are central, the
crowned donor
being presented
by St John the
Evangelist, holding
the red chalice; the
figure of the Virgin
with the infant Christ
to the left presents
Anne d'Egmont.

2

Cardinal Prince
Bishop of Liège Érard
de la Marck is shown
kneeling in a red cope
above a cardinal's hat,
reflecting his status
since 1520. He was
a patron of stained
glass in Brussels
and Liège Cathedral
where St Lambert
(shown here in gold)
is patron saint and,
with the Virgin, the
protector of the city.

3

Before a deep blue
sky, Maximilian
d'Egmont and
Françoise de Lannoy
(at right) face an
altar; he is presented
by St Christopher,
carrying the infant
Christ on his left
shoulder, while St
Barbara accompanies
Françoise de Lannoy.

4

Florent d'Egmont
(centre) and his
wife Marguerite de
Berghes; like his son
Maximilian above,
Florent, dressed in
armour as a Knight
of the Golden
Fleece, is presented
by St Christopher,
showing a familial
relationship to the
saint. Marguerite
is presented by
her dragon-slaying
namesake St Margaret,
a patron of childbirth.

WINDOW NORTH III
SAINTS AND DONORS

1

St Henry, Emperor, and Henry de Lexhy; shield of arms; St Christine and Christine Zelighs.

2

Jean de Mettecoven and St John the Baptist; St John the Evangelist and another figure; Marguerite de Lexhy and St Margaret.

3

Gerard III van Velpen and his son; St Agnes; Agnes de Mettecoven.

4

Charlemagne; the lactation of St Bernard; possibly St Humbeline.

5

Angel holding the arms of Johanna Verhese; donor presented by St John the Evangelist to the Virgin and Child (at right).

6

Virgin and Child; Arms of Beatrice of Lobosh, Abbess of Herkenrode (d. 1371); an abbess with her nuns.

WINDOW NORTH II
THREE SCENES FROM THE LIFE OF CHRIST

1

The Flagellation: this window is difficult to read, but it shows Christ tied to a (green) column with a golden capital, being flogged with twigs and other implements.

2

Crowning with Thorns: the crown is pressed onto Christ's head, as he is given a martyr's palm.

3

The Annunciation: The Virgin in blue sits to the right, the Archangel Gabriel approaches from the left, forming an interesting comparison with the 'Lichfield Angel', seven hundred years on. The two background figures depict the 'Visitation' of Mary to Elizabeth (Mary's cousin and mother of John the Baptist), as told in Luke 1:39–56.

WINDOW I
SCENES FROM THE LIFE OF CHRIST

1

The Ascension: behind groups of the Apostles, Christ rises to heaven flanked by angels, while the Virgin Mary kneels in the foreground.

2

The Road to Emmaus and the Supper at Emmaus (1532): through the left arch is a scene of Christ on the Road to Emmaus; the central section shows Christ at a table flanked by two figures.

3

The Three Marys: the central section showing the Virgin and Child is a replica of that in window NIII; Mary Magdalene and Mary of Cleopas are shown flanking the central figures in a landscape, as if present at the Crucifixion, no doubt the original context.

WINDOW SOUTH II

THREE SCENES FROM THE LIFE OF CHRIST

1

The Last Supper: as Christ and the Apostles sit at a large table beneath a grand red and white arch, Judas is seen leaving to the right, dressed in treasonous yellow.

2

The Entry into Jerusalem: Christ (centre) rides an ass, followed by the Apostles. The gate of first-century Jerusalem improbably carries the date '1538'. Note the man climbing a tree, perhaps to gain a view.

3

The Arrest of Christ: Judas, again wearing yellow, presents a kiss to Christ, who turns to face those who have come to arrest him, on the right.

WINDOW SOUTH III

THREE SCENES FROM THE LIFE OF CHRIST

1

The Last Judgement: Christ shown in glory on an orb, as described in the Book of Revelation; beneath him, figures emerge from their interment as angels sound their trumpets.

2

Pentecost: this scene, dated 1534, shows the Virgin seated centrally, surrounded by the Apostles expressing astonishment at the descent of the Holy Spirit, depicted as flames rising from their heads.

3

The Incredulity of St Thomas: in a beautifully detailed interior space, St Thomas and the Apostles gather around the arisen Christ.

WINDOW SOUTH IV
FOUR SCENES FROM THE LIFE OF CHRIST

1

The Carrying of the Cross: The Virgin in blue is supported by John the Evangelist; St Veronica (in green and russet) holds up the cloth imprinted with Christ's visage, as he carries the burden of the cross surrounded by jeering soldiers. The left column is dated 1532.

2

Christ leaving Pilate: Christ, in purple, is led away by two soldiers as the seated figure of Pilate, in vivid red and blue, washes his hands, referring to St Matthew's assertion that Pilate lobbied to spare Christ from execution. Above a fine asymmetrical townscape, the cartouche is dated 1539.

3

The Descent from the Cross: Christ is lowered from the cross, his (heavily restored) legs supported by St John the Evangelist, while the Virgin gestures with grief.

4

The Resurrection: Christ, in red, rises triumphant, standing on a fine sarcophagus while four guards scramble from the sight; in the background to the right, Christ encounters St Peter.

Notes

1 Hemer, K.A., Evans, J.A., Chenery, C.A., Lamb, A.L., 'Evidence of early medieval trade and migration between Wales and the Mediterranean Sea region', *Journal of Archaeological Science*, Vol. 40, Issue 5 (May 2013), pp. 2352–59, shows post-Roman North African migrants to Wales constituted 20% of sampled remains, explaining the presence of Byzantine pottery in north Cornwall.

2 Analysis of the bones awkwardly concluded that three femurs were included, two of which are from left legs. In 1995 radiocarbon dating estimated the age of all the bones to be seventh century, except one eighth-century femur. This presented the distinct possibility that some of these bones were indeed of St Chad. The Vatican approved them as relics to be venerated collectively.

3 Penda's Christian conversion was a condition for his marriage to Alchflaed, daughter of King Oswiu of Northumbria (642–70), who had succeeded his slain brother Oswald.

4 York's cathedral had been dedicated to St Peter by Oswald in 637 and yet was already apparently dilapidated.

5 '[The plague] appeared initially shortly after an eclipse of the sun on May 1 664, killing both King Earconberht of Kent and Deusdedit, Archbishop of Canterbury on 14 July; in the autumn it was present in Deira, where Bishop Cedd died in his monastery of Lastingham on 23 October.' Dunn (2009), pp. 122–27.

6 Eddius Stephanus, *The Life of Bishop Wilfrid*, ed. Colgrave, B. (Cambridge, 1985), p. 33.

7 'Whilst there may well have been an earlier settlement at Lichfield before Chad's time, none of the evidence thus far considered necessitates that there was, and much that has been thought to do so is less suggestive than might be hoped.' Sargent (2013), p. 4.

8 Northumbrian monks used decorated prayer carpets, known as *oratorii*, which influenced the decorated 'carpet' pages of manuscripts. These are Coptic (Egyptian) in origin, and influenced Islamic prayer mats, which are still in use.

9 Strictly, Wells became a cathedral from 909, but was founded as a minster church in *c*.705 by Ine of Wessex on the site of a mortuary chapel, itself on a Romano-British spring and site of worship.

10 Following the Synod of Whitby in 664, the leading churchmen of northern England pursued a Roman style of architecture, especially those who travelled abroad. Benedict Biscop (*c*.628–90) journeyed to Rome from his stone-built glazed priory at Monkwearmouth in Northumbria. His experience of continental masonry buildings inspired his arched and barrel-vaulted buildings, while another intrepid contemporary who knew Italy, St Wilfred, reused Roman stone to build vaulted crypts at Hexham and Ripon, based on ancient catacombs. The finely sculpted wayside crosses of the Northumbrian hills are some of the highest achievements of European art of this era. They were informed by works of art as distant as the Egyptian and Syrian deserts, and yet communicated the triumph of Christ to native literates through runic script. This outburst of art was a form of appropriated Roman cosmopolitanism, almost certainly combined with the culture of post-Roman Mediterranean settlers in the west of the British Isles, of whom there is more to learn.

11 The choice of phrase is specific, from 1 Peter 2: 5: 'Ye also, as lively stones, are built up a spiritual house, an holy priesthood'. The passage was suited to evangelists who converted a populace to Christianity on behalf of a monarchy: 'But ye *are* a chosen generation, a royal priesthood, an holy nation, a peculiar people; that ye should shew forth the praises of him who hath called you out of darkness into his marvellous light: Which in time past *were* not a people, but are now the people of God' (1 Peter 2: 9–10).

12 'Peter/Petrus' being derived from the Greek *petra*, for 'mass of rock'.

13 'On the evidence of form and art style, the majority of the finds undoubtedly fit with the material culture of the first half of the seventh century. One object, in particular, remains

contentious within the overall dating: the inscribed strip (K550). Okasha has dated it to the eighth century, and Brown dates it no earlier than *c*.650. However, its (empty) gem-setting with filigree collar and zoomorphic surround, and even the niello inlay to its lettering, all indicate manufacture in keeping with other hoard objects.' H.E.M. Cool, http://www.barbicanra.co.uk/assets/pd-appendix-2-typology.pdf, pp. 24–25.

14 *'Surge domine et disepentur inimici tui et fugent qui oderunt te a facie tua'* which should read: *'Surge domine et dissipentur inimici tui et fugiant qui oderunt te a facie tua'*. See http://www.staffordshirehoard.org.uk/staritems/the-biblical-inscription.

15 His contribution has been questioned by Roman-era archaeology. The Romans may well have established a ditch akin to a Hadrian's Wall. But as the dyke was attributed to Offa by Asser in the tenth century, it seems he was deemed substantially responsible for this triumph of coordinated labour, whether by rebuilding or completing what went before.

16 Matthew Paris relates a story of suspect authority, but instructive of Lichfield's repute, that when King Offa was at Bath in about 793, he dreamed of a visitation by an angel, who instructed him to raise the body of St Alban from its obscure grave and put it more fittingly in a shrine. When he awoke, the practical advice Offa sought was that of Archbishop Hygeberht of Lichfield.

17 It is telling of the quality of English intellectual culture, and the ongoing influence of the Celtic church, that Charlemagne's teacher from the 780s was the Northumbrian scholar Alcuin (735–804).

18 'And in the sixth month the angel Gabriel was sent from God unto a city of Galilee, named Nazareth, to a virgin espoused to a man whose name was Joseph, of the house of David; and the virgin's name was Mary. [...] And the angel said unto her, Fear not, Mary: for thou hast found favour with God. And, behold, thou shalt conceive in thy womb, and bring forth a son, and shalt call his name JESUS. And the angel [...] said unto her, The Holy Ghost shall come upon thee, and the power of the Highest shall overshadow thee: therefore also that holy thing which shall be born of thee shall be called the Son of God.' (Luke 1: 26–37)

19 It has traditionally but erroneously been claimed that in 822 Lichfield hosted canons for the first time under Bishop Aethelweald, apparently following the model of Chrodegang of Metz and Canterbury in 813, with eleven priests and nine deacons led by a provost. But C.P. Lewis has shown that it is likelier that its five priests were by then established, 'something well short of a formal chapter living under a rule'.

20 The evidence for this is slight. See Crosby, E., *The Kings' Bishops: The Politics of Patronage in England and Normandy, 1066–1216* (New York, 2013).

21 William of Malmesbury claimed so, but exaggerated it for rhetorical effect as a commentary on episcopal pride expecting more. Lewis (2011), pp. 68–69.

22 He was called 'Bishop of Chester' by 1072, so the Council of London was possibly retrospective. See Lewis (2011), p. 63.

23 Lewis (2011), p. 67.

24 Lichfield's other churches, St Chad's and St Michael's (not yet St Mary's), were still regarded as chapels-of-ease, though St Michael has a substantial and apparently ancient churchyard which in the sixteenth century gave rise to the almost certainly mistaken suspicion that it might have been Chad's church.

25 Lichfield's Sunday market was granted to Bishop Durdent by King Stephen in 1153 (confirmed by Henry II), with a mint to assist the economic expansion of the city.

26 The preference for statutes from Normandy may have been a show of allegiance to the Angevin kingship, as Bishop Roger vigorously defended King Stephen (1135–54) in his dispute against the rival claims of Empress Matilda. Bishop Richard Peche (1161–82) confirmed that 'the institutions of the church of Rouen, on which this church was originally modelled, so far as they are sound and possible, shall be strictly observed, both in choir and chapter, and in the degrees and dignities of the *personae* and the canons'. S.H.C. (1924), p. 13.

27 'A garden enclosed is my sister, my spouse, a spring shut up, a fountain sealed'. (Song of Solomon 4: 12–16)

28 After the 1174 fire, William of Sens at Canterbury adopted the thin walls and skeletal vaults of his native France in tandem with round arches and classical columns, to harmonize with Canterbury's surviving fabric while evoking its Roman origins under St Augustine, its founder sent from Rome in 596. The unknown designer of Wells seemed unfettered by the past, and pioneered a rich, rationally consistent system of shafts and arches applied to thick-walled construction, the capitals decorated with organic 'stiff-leaf' carving.

29 Greenslade (1970). This endowment of Bakewell collegiate church also established a prebend at Lichfield to support a perpetual mass for John's soul, a notably early example of a chantry.

30 Greenslade (1970), p. 143.

31 The Civil War saw the cisterns and pipes within the cathedral close dug up and sold; the continuation of supply consequently depended on repairs. The Conduit Head was listed Grade II* only in 1988: 'Conduit head. Probably mid-C12. Large sandstone blocks, part refaced to lower parts in brick; solid stone roofing blocks. A small square gabled structure set into a bank so that only the gable and the roof are visible; small central (probably C19) entrance with boarded door. The interior has a pointed vault and drops below ground level (the water level was found to be 2m off the floor in 1975) to the water basin in which the lead conduit was fed. The conduit served Lichfield Cathedral and was originally instigated in 1166, used continuously until 1969 when it was abandoned. The conduit head (q.v.) and basin (q.v.) are still visible in the close.' (Listing NGR: SK0923009280).

32 See Richard of Devizes' chronicle and discussion in Bartlett, R.C., *England Under the Norman and Angevin Kings: 1075–1225* (Oxford, 2000), p. 477.

33 Pennant, quoted in *Dodsley's Annual Register* (1782), p. 130.

34 Intendedly for its founder Remigius (d. 1093), but eventually celebrating its canonised rebuilder St Hugh (d. 1200). The fact that Lincoln was once within Chad's territory of Lindsey may have been known to Lichfield's new bishop and Dean Mancetter.

35 Stavensby taught theology at Toulouse and visited Rome in 1226 and 1234, Gascony in 1235.

36 See Foyle, J., *Architecture of Canterbury Cathedral* (London, 2013).

37 A slightly later form of funerary monument can be found on the south aisle of the nave and the choir, showing shallow-relief sculpted effigies of heads and feet framed within separate panels, either side of a plain panel in lieu of an abdomen. What can explain them? Perhaps this: Bede had recorded an ethos of burial very specific to Lichfield in the time of St Chad, when plague 'through the death of the body, translated the living stones of the church from their earthly sites to the heavenly building'. Bede's metaphorical account of the burials of the founders of the church, as stones of this heavenly building, looks to have been taken literally by those who upheld its traditions and authority. See the similar example of Nicholas Hyde at All Saints, Standon, dated 1511.

38 Bodl. MS. Top. Eccl. d. 6, f. 13v.

39 Thomas Pennant's eye failed him in reading this, which remained where Stukeley had seen it 80 years on: 'IN St. *Mary's* chapel is a fragment of singular sculpture, of two gothic arches: beneath one is a king sitting, with one hand on a young prince; beneath the other a monarch also seated.'

40 This stacked spatial arrangement was reversed at Wells Cathedral after 1280.

41 The relationship is clear: Lincoln's richly detailed entrance façade, originally facing into a timber pentice, is one of the few structures whose arches compare with Lichfield's chapter house entrance, while Lichfield's choice of Y-shaped tracery had one known source in the 1240s – Lincoln's consistory court and possibly the nave's great west window.

42 Avranches (1986), p. 61.

43 Lichfield's chapter house could conceivably relate to this culture of Roman emulation, if a Lincolnshire bishop imported current knowledge, or if the *Metrical Life of St Hugh* was read at Lichfield. But to explain Lichfield's variances from both the Pantheon and Lincoln admittedly requires special pleading. Though the main volume of the Pantheon is indeed a single space, its entry is flanked by stairs to an upper chamber of the vestibule, while it may be argued that the total volume contained beneath Lichfield's upper chamber vault better represents the Pantheon's length-to-height proportions than Lincoln managed to achieve in its single volume. The most curious feature of the Lichfield chapter house plan is the elongation of the octagon into a slight west-east axis. This would have retained the essentially octagonal form while mitigating the problem of totally centralized spaces, which created an equivalency for all those looking inward from an encircling stone bench that defied the primacy of the dean's seat beneath the east window.

44 See Kellet (1990).

45 This appearing in the transcript of the fifteenth-century Chapter Act Book, see Swanson (2004).

46 There is a further comparable example on the northern crossing pier into Durham Cathedral's Chapel of Nine Altars, indicating a common source for these creatures that may have originated here. That they symbolized evil is clear; at Durham they accompany a tortured face, while at the southern choir aisle portal into Lincoln's Angel Choir, a robed figure who is almost certainly St Hugh stabs them through the mouth as they attempt to eat grapes symbolic of Christ's blood. They share space with two huddled owls symbolizing Jewry, blamed for the death of the boy 'Little St Hugh' in 1255. Wells Cathedral's grape-eating dragon is relatable but different in character to this group.

47 Westminster's masons carved faceted, then brightly coloured, blocks above the main arcades of the eastern arm, overlooking the Confessor's shrine. Lincoln Cathedral featured busts in the arcades of the choir aisles in the 1190s. Wells' west front is an array of quatrefoils and gables, which, historians have recently argued, evoked shrines

48 Trefoils, quatrefoils and cinquefoils were used together in the gable over the Judgment Portal at Lincoln. As this also represents the theme of Christ's wounds and blood sacrifice, which would emerge at Lichfield in its wake, the consistency is striking. Perhaps the trinity, four evangelists and five wounds were in the minds of the makers.

49 Mary remained the great protectress, and it is no coincidence that the chapel built for the soldiers garrisoned at Caernarvon was also dedicated to her.

50 Daniel King's engraving shows as much. This arrangement would have been synergistic with Mary as the stem of the Tree of Jesse, beneath Christ.

51 Tempting as it is, toponyms were too common for family shame to account for Walter Peverel's preference for 'Langton'.

52 Canterbury's Lambeth Palace remains to the south of the river, and Winchester's palace ruins can be found in Southwark, while 'Lincoln's Inn' and 'Ely Place' are to the north-east.

53 Lyte, H.C.M., ed., *Calendar of Patent Rolls 1301–7* (1898), p. 367.

54 See Binski (1986).

55 'In the first place, the head of Blessed Chad in a certain painted wooden case. Also an arm of Blessed Chad. Also bones of the said Saint in a certain portable shrine.' Then the 'great shrine'.

56 Crook (2011), p. 80.

57 Cox (1886).

58 Binski (2014) argues that Ely's Lady Chapel, at 30 x 15 m (100 x 50 ft) internally shared the proportions of the Temple of Solomon, at 100 x 50 cubits. This seems numerically significant, but the overlooked and slightly earlier proportional coincidence at Lichfield disrupts the logic of that argument, unless Ely is a further refinement. The shaft-niches and nodding ogee arcades are also worth further comparison, as they also happen at Lichfield first.

59 Though according to Le Neve (1964), he lasted less than seven months before reverting to a canon.

60 Northborough is close to the Jurassic limestone quarries of Barnack, near Stamford, which supplied many of the great abbeys of eastern England, such as Peterborough, Crowland and Thorney, scores of village churches, and other fine medieval houses such as Longthorpe Tower, whose early fourteenth-century wall paintings hint at the interiors Northburgh knew.

61 International financial relationships and the wool trade fostered a cultural exchange between fourteenth-century England and Italy, especially Florence and Rome. The influence of Italian art has been noted at Norwich and Ely in this period. But Lichfield seems to have been more heavily populated with Italians than either; it followed Coventry in appointing a string of Latin clerics in the first half of the fourteenth century. At

Lichfield, some were precentors: Raymond de Got (Raimondo di Gotti?), 1307–10; Odo de Colonna, 1310–11; and Anibaldus Gaetani de Ceccano, cardinal bishop of Tusculum (1343–40). William de Bosco was chancellor, 1310–29, and Lichfield also had an Italian treasurer in Hugh Pelegrini, 1348–70. Together with his brother Raimondo, Hugh was a papal tax collector in England for over 20 years.

62 This novelty did not harm his reputation, as he became a commissioner for the Tower of London and surveyor of the king's castles south of the Trent. He built the principal stage of St Stephen's Chapel in Westminster Palace, based on the Sainte-Chapelle, and he is sometimes credited with the remodelling of Gloucester Abbey's choir after it received the burial of Edward II in 1327.

63 Comparable with Lincoln's 'Bishop's Eye' of 1338, and the transepts of St Mary Redcliffe in Bristol.

64 This deduction was made by R.N. Swanson (2004) further researched by Carole Goulding, pers. comm., to whom I am grateful.

65 Lichfield is the only cathedral known to have had a burial that included a consecrated host, found under the nave south arcade. Rodwell (2005), p. 205.

66 Five-petalled flowers were usually thus associated in the later Middle Ages.

67 See Greenslade (1990), pp. 37–42. 'By the mid 13th century […] the first known attempts to explain "Lichfield" were made. The first element was taken to be "lich" or "liches" and the place name to mean "the field of corpses", which needed an explanation' but 'the story was not taken seriously in medieval Lichfield. There is no evidence of any cult of the martyrs.' I beg to differ.

68 Lydgate (1974).

69 '*Hi sunt, qui venerunt de tribulatione magna, et laverant Stolas suas, et delabaverunt eas in sanguine agnis/ Laus martyrii in causa bonitatis, non in poenae acerbitate/ Ad praesides et reges ducemini in testimonium illis et gentibus/ Ecclesia semen sanguis Martyrum.*' Recorded in Lomax & Newling, (1819), pp. 6–7. I am grateful to Professor Sally McKee for translating as: 'These are the ones who came from great tribulation and washed their mantles and dipped them in the blood of the lamb/ Praise the martyr's grave for the sake of goodness, not in the bitterness of punishment/ To the preeminent and kings you are led in witness to them and the people/ The Church is the seed of the blood of the Martyrs.'

70 Camm, Dom B., *Forgotten Shrines: An Account of Some Old Catholic Halls and Families in England and of Relics and Memorials of the English Martyrs* (London, 1910), pp. 73–74, explains the recusant Catholic Fitzherbert family's role in preserving the figure, which is 'pointing to the wound in His Sacred Heart'. Gerald Cobb (1980) picked this up.

71 As did the seated Christ in the Judgment Portal at Lincoln show his spear wound; as Lincoln's masons built Lichfield's nave, we may make some further speculation here about the integrity of vision intended for the nave and west front from *c*.1257.

72 See Vincent (2001). Remarkably, no mention is made of Lichfield, nor does holy blood feature in any other account of its medieval identity.

73 The procession of the Holy Blood at Bruges was a late thirteenth-century development, on Ascension Day.

74 See aisle bosses and portals at Lincoln's Angel Choir in the context of the martyred Little St Hugh (d. 1255), explained in Foyle (2015).

75 'An investigation of the roof proved that its bosses had been originally profusely gilded and painted, and that the ribs had been painted in tri-colour, though, oddly enough, not in the Lady Chapel.' After an abortive attempt to repaint them under Dyce, 'what little paint had been applied to the ribs was removed; but a few of the more easterly bosses remain gilt to this day, and afterwards the others were reddened to bring out the sculpture'. Clifton (1898), p. 76.

76 *The Golden Legend* describes the Virgin's preparation for death on a bed, whereupon her soul ascended while her body was taken to the valley of Josaphat. See Voraigne, *The Golden Legend*, Vol. II, p. 80.

77 For example, Pevsner (1974): 'The transept vaults are a later renewal, whether *c*.1300N and after 1350S or both late C15 does not seem certain.' The late C15 attribution may have been the result of mistaking the Marian roses as 'Tudor'.

78 Greenslade (1970), p. 158, n. 92, quoting Lichfield Diocesan Registry, B/A/1/3, f.127.

79 When Northburgh spoke of modernizing, he surely had the bright new choir in mind, but his metropolitan experience knew an even fresher wonder, made for Edward III. Under Ramsey's guidance, the main vault at the luminous (and much-crenellated) St Stephen's Chapel, Westminster, was being completed; the shaft capitals and a carved bust of a king high in the south transept may refer to this modern royal relationship.

80 Maddison (1993), p. 76.

81 Southworth (2012), p. 27.

82 Savage (1925), though the claim is ill-referenced.

83 Swanson (1989), pp. 142 & 153. The year has been questioned, as the author claims 22 May 1445 was not a Friday – but it was. And the description of 'consort' rather than 'queen' supports an even earlier date than the marriage; the entry follows one of 1444, the year 1445 is repeated by the transcriber, and the transcription names the sacrist as Robert Godioborn, whose name is recorded as a vicar choral in 1447.

84 Swanson (2004).

85 Harwood (1806), p. 112: 'An ancient painting was discovered in the south aile, upon the wall of the cathedral, under the whitewash, by the late Rev. Theophilus Buckeridge, Master of St. John's Hospital in this city. From a mutilated inscription in old court-hand, it is supposed to have been put up by Oliver De Langton, rector of Wyggan in 1450.' An Oliver De Langton who financially supported the cathedral in 1451 is also found in G.T.O. Bridgman, *The History of the Church & Manor of Wigan* (Chetham Society, Manchester 1888), p. 69.

86 Nilson (1998), p. 139; a list of 50,000 names recorded by A.J. Kettle, 'A list of the families in the archdeaconry of Stafford, 1532–3', *Staffs Rec. Soc.*, 4th Series, viii (1976), pp. vii–xi, is accepted by Lepine (1995), p. 16, but whether it relates to Lichfield's guilds is 'open to speculation', according to R.N. Swanson, 'Books of brotherhood: registering fraternity and confraternity in late medieval England', in Rollason, D.W., ed., *The Durham Liber Vitae and its Context* (Woodbridge 2004), p. 244. No confirmed membership register is known for any cathedral confraternity.

87 See Warwick Rodwell's account of the Vicars' Close in Hall, R., & Stocker, D. (2005), pp. 61–75,

explaining fourteenth-century origins and with the lodgings representing mid- to late-fifteenth-century construction in three stages.

88 Set out in Storer's history (1817).

89 Says Pennant.

90 Anthony Wood, *Athenae Oxonienses*, Vol. 2 (1815), pp. 433–34.

91 Fox, G. 'A Sense of the Blood of Martyrs' from his *Journal*, in Craik, H., ed., *English Prose* (London, 1917). Fox knew what the cathedrals' spires were, of course, but previous readings have overlooked his use of the cathedral's own association with martyrdom to denounce the more recent examples in the Market Place. In the 1550s, during the reign of Mary, Thomas Hayward, John Goreway and Joyce Lewis were burned at the stake. In 1612 Edward Wightman was convicted of heresy and similarly burned, the last person so to die in England.

92 Thomas Pennant (1783), p. 110, claims to have seen a manuscript of costs for the rebuilding that 'makes the sum much less' than the usually quoted £20,000.

93 Clifton (1898), p. 84.

94 Stone (1870), p. 66.

95 Woodhouse & Newling (1870), p. 60.

96 James (2009), p. 16.

97 Pevsner (1974), p. 177.

98 Lockett (1993), pp. 123–24.

Sources and Select Bibliography

No works accounts survive for medieval Lichfield Cathedral. The excellent Staffordshire *Victoria County History* volumes (see 'Greenslade', ed.) remain an unrivalled resource for the city and cathedral, and have informed much of this book. Also important for architectural analyses are the studies comprising the *British Archaeological Association Conference Transactions XIII: Medieval Archaeology and Architecture at Lichfield* (1993) called 'BAA 1993' below. Warwick Rodwell's careful archaeological analyses for the dean and chapter fill out the picture for more recent investigations.

The following is a select bibliography of sources that offer particular insights.

ABINGDON, T., *Some Short Account of the Cathedral Church of Lichfield*, Lichfield Cathedral Library MS 22

AVRANCHES, H., ed. GARTON, C., *The Metrical Life of St Hugh* (Lincoln, 1986)

BEDE, *The Ecclesiastical History of the English People*, eds McClure, J., Collins, R.; transl. Colgrave, B. (Oxford, 2008)

BINSKI, P., *The Painted Chamber at Westminster*, Society of Antiquaries Occasional Paper (New Series) IX (London, 1986)

BINSKI, P., *Gothic Wonder: Art, Artifice and the Decorated Style, 1290–1350* (London and New Haven, 2014)

BROWN, M.P., *The Lindisfarne Gospels: Society, Spirituality and the Scribe*, Vol. 1 (Toronto, 2003)

CAVE, C.P., *Roof Bosses in Medieval Churches: An Aspect of Gothic Sculpture* (Cambridge, 1948)

CLIFTON, A.B., *The Cathedral Church of Lichfield, A Description of its Fabric and a Brief History of the Episcopal See* (London, 1898)

COBB, G., *English Cathedrals: The Forgotten Centuries* (London, 1980)

COCKE, T., 'Ruin and Restoration: Lichfield Cathedral in the Seventeenth Century', BAA, 1993, pp. 109–14

COHEN, M., *The Sainte-Chapelle and the Construction of Sacral Monarchy: Royal Architecture in Thirteenth-Century Paris* (Cambridge, 2014)

COLDSTREAM, N., *The Decorated Style: Architecture and Ornament, 1240–1360* (Toronto, 1994)

COOL, H.E.M., 'Contextualising Metal-Detected Discoveries: Staffordshire Anglo-Saxon Hoard', Barbican Research Associates Project 5892, Stage 2 Project Design v4, 9 January 2015

COX, J.C., ed., 'Sacrist's Roll of Lichfield Cathedral Church A.D. 1345', *Collections for a History of Staffordshire*, Vol. 6, Part 2, Appendix 1, 1886, pp. 199–221

CROOK, J., *English Medieval Shrines* (Woodbridge, 2011)

DEFOE, D., *A Tour Through the Whole Island of Great Britain [etc]*, Vol. II, Letter III (1725 et seq.)

DUGDALE, W., and CALEY, W., ed., *Monasticon Anglicanum [etc]*, Vol. 6, Issue 3 (London, 1849), pp. 1238–1266

DUNN, M., *The Christianization of the Anglo-Saxons c.597–c.700* (London, 2009)

EDWARDS, K., *The English Secular Cathedrals in the Middle Ages* (Manchester, 1949)

FOYLE, J., *Lincoln Cathedral: The Biography of a Great Building* (London, 2015)

FREW, J.M., 'Cathedral Improvements: James Wyatt at Lichfield Cathedral, 1787–92' *South Staffordshire Archaeological and Historical Society*, Vol. XIX (1977–78), pp. 33–40

GITTOS, H., *Liturgy, Architecture and Sacred Places in Anglo-Saxon England* (Oxford, 2013)

GOULD, J., 'Pre-Conquest Finds Made During the 19th century at Lichfield', *South Staffordsshire Archaeological and Historical Society*, Vol. XVIII (1976–77)

GOULD, J., 'The Twelfth-Century Water Supply to Lichfield Close', *The Antiquaries Journal*, LVI, Part I (1976), pp. 73–9

GOULD, J., 'Lichfield Before St Chad' (BAA, 1993), pp. 1–10

GREENSLADE, M.W., and PUGH, R.B., eds *Victoria County History: A History of the County of Stafford: Volume III* (London, 1970), the section on Lichfield Cathedral (pp. 139–99) by KETTLE, A. and JOHNSON, S.A. published as an offprint in 1982 by Staffordshire County Library

GREENSLADE, M.W., *Victoria County History: A History of the County of Stafford: Volume XI*, (London, 1990), pp. xv–xvi. Available online at http://www.british-history.ac.uk/vch/staffs/vol14/xv-xvi [accessed 16 October 2015]

HALL, R., & STOCKER, D., eds, *Vicars Choral at English Cathedrals* Cantate Domino *History, Architecture and Archaeology* (Oxford, 2005)

HARVEY, J.H., *English Medieval Architects: A Biographical Dictionary down to 1550* (Gloucester, 1984)

HARWOOD, T., *The History and Antiquities of the Church and City of Lichfield* (Gloucester, 1806)

JAMES, H., *Cathedrals and Castles* (London, 2009)

JENKINS, H.T., *Lichfield Cathedral in the Fourteenth Century*, unpublished B. Litt thesis, University of Oxford, 1956

KELLETT, A., 'King John's Maundy', *History Today*, Vol. 40, Issue 4 (April 1990)

KETTLE, A.J., 'City and Close: Lichfield in the Century before the Reformation' in HARPER-BILL, C., and BARRON, C., eds, *The Church in Pre-Reformation Society: Essays in Honour of F.R.H. DuBoulay* (Woodbridge, Suffolk, 1985), pp. 158–69

LEHMBERG, S., *Cathedrals Under Siege: Cathedrals in English Society, 1600–1700* (University Park Pennsylvania, 1996)

LE NEVE, J., ed., *Fasti Ecclesiae Anglicanae 1300–1541, X: Coventry and Lichfield Diocese* (London, 1964)

LEWIS, C.P., 'Communities, Conflict and Episcopal Policy in the Diocese of Lichfield, 1050–1150' in *Cathedrals, Communities and Conflict in the Anglo-Norman World*, eds DALTON, P., INSLEY, C., & WILKINSON, L. (Woodbridge, 2011)

LOCKETT, R., 'The Restoration of Lichfield Cathedral: James Wyatt to John Oldrid Scott', BAA, 1993, pp. 115–39

LOMAX, T.G, & Newling, W., *A Short Account of the City and Close of Lichfield (etc)* (Lichfield, 1819)

LYDGATE, J., in van der Westhuizen, J.E., ed., *The Life of Saint Alban and Saint Amphibal* (Leiden, 1974)

MADDISON, J., 'Building at Lichfield During the Episcopate of Walter Langton (1296–1321)', BAA 1993, pp. 65–84

MORRIS, R.K., 'The Lapidary Collections of Lichfield Cathedral', BAA 1993, pp. 101–108

NILSON, B. *Cathedral Shrines of Medieval England* (Woodbridge, 1998)

PENNANT, T., *The Journey from Chester to London* (Dublin, 1783)

PEVSNER, N., *The Buildings of England: Staffordshire* (Harmondsworth, 1974)

RODWELL, W., 'The Development of the Choir of Lichfield Cathedral: Romanesque and Early English', BAA 1993, pp. 17–35

RODWELL, W., 'Archaeology and the Standing Fabric: Recent Studies at Lichfield Cathedral', in *The Archaeology of Cathedrals*, eds TATTON-BROWN, T., and MUNBY, J. (Oxford, 1996), pp. 81–94

RODWELL, W., 'The Forgotten Cathedral', *Current Archaeology*, Vol. XVIII. No. 205 (Sept/Oct 2005), pp. 8–17

RODWELL, W., Archaeological reports deposited at Lichfield Cathedral Library include:

▸ *The Norman and Early Gothic Quires of Lichfield Cathedral: An Archaeological Study* (5 May 1987)

▸ *Saint Chad's Shrine, Lichfield Cathedral: Notes on the Evidence for its Site and Construction* (10 November 1990)

▸ *Saint Chad's Shrine, Lichfield Cathedral: Notes on the Archaeological Potential of its Site* (1 February 1991)

▸ *An Interim Report on Archaeological Investigations in the Nave of Lichfield Cathedral* (30 January 2000)

▸ *Archaeological Excavation in the Nave of Lichfield Cathedral, 2003* (4 November 2003)

▸ *Lichfield Cathedral: Interim report on Archaeological Excavations in the North Quire Aisle, Aug–Sept 1994* (20 September 1994)

SARGENT, A., 'Early Medieval Lichfield: A Reassessment', *Staffordshire Archaeological and Historical Society Transactions*, Vol. 46, 2013, pp. 1–32

SAVAGE, The Very Rev. H.E., ed., *Collections for a history of Staffordshire: Magnum Registrum Album* (Kendal, 1924)

SAVAGE, The Very Rev. H.E., *Dean Thomas Heywode* (Lichfield, 1925)

SAVAGE, The Very Rev. H.E., 'A Secular Cathedral under Henry VIII and Edward VI', *Theology*, Vol. XVI, February 1928, pp. 63–71

SOUTHWORTH, C.M., *The Canons of Lichfield Cathedral in the Last Quarter of the Fifteenth Century* M.Phil thesis, University of Birmingham, 2012

SPURRELL, Rev. M., 'The Procession of Palms and West-front Galleries', *The Downside Review*, April 2001, pp. 125–44

STONE, J.B., *A History of Lichfield Cathedral from its Foundation to the Present Time [etc]* (1870)

STUDD, R., 'Pre-Conquest Lichfield', *South Staffordshire Archaeological and Historical Society*, Vol. XXII (1980–1), pp. 24–33

SWANSON, R.N., *Church and Society in Late Medieval England* (Oxford, 1989)

SWANSON, R.N., 'Extracts from a fifteenth-century Lichfield Cathedral Chapter Act Book', *Staffordshire Record Society* 2004, pp. 129–70

THURLBY, M., 'The Early Gothic Transepts of Lichfield Cathedral', BAA 1993, pp. 50–64

TRINGHAM, N., 'The Palace of Walter Langton in Lichfield Cathedral Close', BAA 1993, pp. 85–100

VANDEN BEMDEN, Y., & KERR, J., 'The Sixteenth-Century Glass from Herkenrode Abbey (Belgium) in Lichfield Cathedral', *Archaeologia*, Vol. CVIII (1986), pp. 189–226

VINCENT, N., *The Holy Blood: King Henry III and the Westminster Blood Relic* (Cambridge, 2001)

De VORAIGNE, J., *The Golden Legend: Readings on the Saints*, transl. RYAN, W.G., 2 vols (Princeton, 1993)

WILLIS, Rev. R , 'Memoir of the Foundations of Early Buildings, recently discovered in Lichfield Cathedral', *Archaeological Journal*, XVIII (1861), reprinted by the Archaeological Institute MDCCCLXI

WOODHOUSE, J.C., & NEWLING, W., *A Short Account of Lichfield Cathedral*, 9th edn (Lichfield, 1870)

Index

SIZE2 NA5471 .L5 F69 2016

Foyle, Jonathan

Lichfield Cathedral

This edition copyright © Scala Arts & Heritage
Publishers Ltd, 2016
Text copyright © Jonathan Foyle 2016
Illustrations copyright © Lichfield Cathedral
2016 except as detailed in the picture credits list

First published in 2016 by
Scala Arts & Heritage Publishers Ltd
10 Lion Yard, Tremadoc Road,
London SW4 7NQ, UK
www.scalapublishers.com

In association with
Lichfield Cathedral, The Close, Lichfield,
Staffordshire WS13 7LD

ISBN 978-1-85751-027-4

Edited by Jessica Hodge
Designed by Andrew Barron
Index by Jane Horton
Printed in China

DATE DUE

All rights reserved. No part of this book may
be reproduced, stored in a retrieval system
... by any means
... opying, recording
... en permission of
... rs Ltd.

... acknowledge
... ere applicable.
... intentional and
... sher, who will
... ar in any reprints.

GAYLORD   PRINTED IN U.S.A.

ILLUSTRATION CREDITS
With special thanks to the Lichfield Cathedral
Photographers team, particularly Richard Ell and
Christopher Lockwood

Photos by Paul Barker © Archbishops' Council:
front cover, pp. 4/5, 8, 9, 26, 59, 72 top, 76, 94, 109,
112/13

Lichfield Cathedral Photographers: back cover,
inside front cover, inside back cover, inside back
flap, pp. 1, 2, 10/11, 12, 25, 30, 32 right, 41 both,
43/4, 44, 45, 46, 47 all, 48 all, 49 both, 51 left above
and below, 52 top, 54, 56/7, 60/1, 66, 67, 68 all, 70
both, 72 below, 73, 77 both, 78 all, 80 both, 81, 82/3,
84, 87, 88, 90, 91, 92/3, 96, 100, 101, 102, 103, 104,
105, 106, 107 all, 108 all

Steve Johnson: p. 7

Fr Lawrence Lew OP: p.14

Dr Jonathan Foyle: pp. 15, 19, 22/3, 28/9, 34, 37, 40,
50, 51 right, 56 right, 58 both, 62, 63, 65, 71, 79, 85,
86

St Mary's church, Reculver: p. 16 left

© Birmingham Museums Trust:
p. 20 both

Photo by Terry Ball (English Heritage Graphics
Team) © Historic England (ref J020158): p. 35

Italy, Padua, Civic Museum 1407: p. 36 left

© British Library Board (155727): p. 36 right

Andy Marshall: pp. 39, 110

Jim Newton: p. 55

Barley Studio, with post production by KIK-
IRPA: pp. 115–19 all

GENERAL THEOLOGICAL SEMINARY
NEW YORK